DEPARTMENTAL COMMITTEE ON THE ADOPTION OF CHILDREN

MEMBERSHIP

Sir William Houghton (Chairman) (Died on 16 November 1971)	Education Officer, Inner London Education Authority
His Honour Judge F A Stockdale (Appointed Chairman on 1 December 1971)	Circuit Judge, Westminster County Court
Mr Leo Abse	Member of Parliament
Mr W K Angus	Clerk to the Reading Justices
Mrs Margaret E Bramall OBE, JP	Director of the National Council for the Unmarried Mother and her Child
Sheriff W J Bryden CBE	Sheriffdom of Lanark
Dr Christine Cooper OBE	Consultant Paediatrician, Department of Child Health, University of Newcastle upon Tyne
Mrs Iris Goodacre	Area Director of Social Services, Oxfordshire
Mrs Hilary Halpin JP	General Secretary of the National Children Adoption Association
The Very Reverend Canon P Harvey	Administrator of the Crusade of Rescue
Mr P Hughes DSC	Director of Social Services, West Riding of Yorkshire
Miss Janet Lusk OBE	Director of the Guild of Service, Edinburgh
Miss Evelyn M Magness	Secretary, Church of England Committee for Social Work and Social Services
Councillor Mrs Dora K Mitchell (Died on 28 February 1972)	Glamorgan County Council
Miss Jane Rowe	Director of the Association of British Adoption Agencies
Dr F H Stone	Consultant Child Psychiatrist, Royal Hospital for Sick Children, Glasgow
Dame Joan Vickers DBE	Member of Parliament
Mr D T White	Director of Social Services, Coventry

iii

Assessors

Mr D H Morrell — Died on 10 December 1969 ⎫
Mr A D Gordon-Brown — (July 1969 to April 1971) ⎬ Home Office
Mr R W Mott — (from April 1971) ⎭

Miss J D Cooper CB ⎫ Department of Health
Mr E W Whittemore MM — (from September 1971) ⎬ and Social Security

Miss P A Cox — (July 1969 to October 1971) ⎫
Mr A F Reid — (from November 1971) ⎬ Social Work Services
Miss M M McInnes ⎬ Group, Edinburgh
Mr D Bennet — (alternate) ⎭

Joint Secretaries

Miss M M Peck — Home Office
Mrs P Roberts — Department of Health and Social Security

HOME OFFICE

SCOTTISH EDUCATION DEPARTMENT

Report of the Departmental Committee on the Adoption of Children

*Presented to Parliament by the Secretary of State for the Home Department
and the Secretary of State for Scotland
by Command of Her Majesty
October 1972*

LONDON
HER MAJESTY'S STATIONERY OFFICE

Cmnd. 5107

"The estimated costs of the preparation of this Report (including the expenses of the Committee) is £9,570 of which £3,765 represents the estimated cost of the printing and publishing of this Report."

SBN 10 151070 5

FOREWORD

As members of a large committee, we began work in the summer of 1969 with gaps in our understanding of adoption problems. The information and advice that came to us as our work progressed added much to our knowledge and we are grateful to those who wrote to us, submitted memoranda, carried out research or gave evidence at our meetings in London and Edinburgh. We listened with interest and advantage to many opinions and now make unanimous recommendations. This is the best tribute we can pay to those who have helped us.

Our thanks are due to our Assessors and Joint Secretaries and the small staff who supported them. Our Assessors changed as time went on and we cannot mention everybody. The untimely death of Mr D H Morrell in December 1969 deprived us of an adviser from whom we had reason to expect much help. During the past three years Miss J D Cooper has given us the benefit of her wide experience of adoption law and practice. Miss M M McInnes has worked with us from the beginning and provided continuity on the Scottish side. Mr A D Gordon-Brown and Miss P A Cox gave us considerable help when we were preparing the working paper issued in 1970. We are obliged to Mr R W Mott for careful advice and much other help he gave us in connection with key chapters in this Report. Mr A F Reid gave us the special information we needed from Scotland and Mr E Whittemore similarly helped us with matters concerning the Department of Health and Social Security.

Our Joint Secretaries, Miss M M Peck and Mrs P Roberts have served the Committee since its first meeting. Our thanks are due to them for their unfailing patience and the skill with which they drafted the working paper and this Report. We were assisted by the papers they wrote for us and their methodical marshalling of the documentary evidence we had to study. Helped by Mr T C Morris, the summaries they made of the oral evidence and the minutes they kept of our meetings were invaluable.

It should be made clear that the recommendations we are making depend upon our own decisions and the judgment we brought to bear upon the problems we hope we have done something to solve.

CONTENTS

REPORT OF THE DEPARTMENTAL COMMITTEE ON THE ADOPTION OF CHILDREN

To The Rt Hon Robert Carr MP, Secretary of State for the Home Department and The Rt Hon Gordon Campbell MC MP, Secretary of State for Scotland.

CHAPTER 1

INTRODUCTION

1. We were appointed on 21 July 1969 by your predecessors to consider the law, policy and procedure on the adoption of children and what changes are desirable. We were asked to interpret these terms of reference fairly broadly and to consider such issues as whether relatives should be able to apply for guardianship instead of adoption, the relation between adoption law and that part of guardianship law which gives the natural father of an illegitimate child the right to apply for guardianship, and in particular the position of long-term foster parents who wish to keep a child permanently, by adoption or otherwise, against the will of the natural parent.

2. Sir William Houghton was appointed to be our Chairman and he presided over our meetings most ably and conscientiously until the day before his sudden death last November. We take this opportunity of paying tribute to the great contribution he made to our work and the concern he showed for the welfare of children. On 1 December 1971 you appointed His Honour Judge F A Stockdale to succeed Sir William as Chairman. We lost another member by the death last February of Councillor Mrs Dora K Mitchell of the Glamorgan County Council, who, despite ill-health, had taken a keen interest in our work.

3. For some time prior to our appointment the Home Office and the Social Work Services Group of the Scottish Education Department had been collecting information from those concerned with adoption work about the way in which adoption law was working and ideas for its improvement. Two research projects, one statistical[1] and one a study of adoption based on a sample of adopted children born in 1958[2] had been undertaken. A major review of adoption practice had been completed by a Committee of the Advisory Councils on Child Care for England and Wales and for Scotland, which prepared "A Guide to Adoption Practice".[3] It was not our function to duplicate this work, but adoption law cannot be considered without regard to the social work and medical services which operate in this field since law and practice are inextricably interwoven.

4. Thus when we were appointed a great deal of information had already been collected. We proceeded, on the basis of this information and the knowledge of our members, to draw up a working paper[4] containing

propositions as a basis for discussion. This was published in October 1970. We made it clear that the working paper did not represent our final or unanimous views. From the outset it was our intention to keep an open mind on all issues until we had fully considered the whole of the evidence given to us.

5. When the working paper was published, all those interested in adoption were invited to send us their comments. We expected that in this way we should obtain a more useful response than by inviting evidence at large. This expectation was amply fulfilled, both by the number of organisations and individuals who responded, and the quality of the evidence we received.

6. After we had received the greater part of the written evidence we took oral evidence, in 48 sessions, from representatives of 40 organisations and 16 individuals. We found these discussions with our witnesses of great value in helping us to assess the many proposals put to us. A list of the sources of our evidence is given in Appendix A.

7. Meanwhile we had commissioned research on the attitude of natural mothers to the adoption process in two areas in England[5] and one in Scotland,[6] a survey of the views of a representative sample of adopters[2] on certain of the provisional proposals, and a study of the use made in Scotland of the provision in Scottish adoption law for an adopted person to have access to his original birth record.[7] We obtained information from a random sample of local authorities about the problems of long-term foster children,* and we had a survey made by the National Children's Bureau of all the relevant research undertaken in adoption and closely related fields. Further reference will be made to some of these studies later in our report.

8. In the light of this evidence, including the comments made on our working paper, the literature we have studied, and the results of research, we now submit our report.

Terminology

For the sake of brevity we refer to the child as "he", and where we refer to a natural parent we often say "the mother" and "she", although we appreciate that in some cases what we say may apply also to the father. The Adoption Act 1958 is referred to as the "1958 Act", and "the court" means any court with jurisdiction to make adoption orders. There is provision for the appointment of a guardian ad litem of the infant in England and Wales and of a curator ad litem in Scotland; for convenience, references to the guardian ad litem include the curator ad litem except where otherwise stated. References to adoption agencies generally include both voluntary societies registered as adoption agencies and local authorities which participate in arrangements for the adoption of children. We refer to a person with whom a child is placed expressly for adoption as a "prospective adopter" or an "applicant for an adoption order", and to other persons who care for children unrelated to them as "foster parents".

---

* Appendix D.

CHAPTER 2

THE BACKGROUND TO ADOPTION TODAY

Historical background

9. The history of adoption in this country up to 1954 was given in some detail in the report of the Hurst Committee.[8] For ease of reference we briefly recapitulate it here and bring the story up to date.

10. Informal adoption had long been practised as a means of helping relatives and friends who could not look after their own children. After the first world war, which left so many children fatherless, it was realised that these informal arrangements did not provide proper security for the child, who did not become a full member of his new family, or for the adopters, who feared that the mother might reclaim the child when he was old enough to earn; or for the mother, who might be called upon to resume the care of the child at any time if the adopters tired of their responsibility for him. This created a demand for legal adoption, which was already available in some other British territories, Australia, for example, having introduced legal adoption in the nineteenth century.

11. A committee under the chairmanship of Sir Alfred Hopkinson KC reported in 1921[9] in favour of legal adoption, and several Bills were introduced with a view to implementing this recommendation. None succeeded and, in view of the divergence of views expressed, a further committee was appointed with Mr Justice Tomlin as Chairman. This Committee reported[10] in 1925 on that part of its terms of reference which related to the adoption of children, and in its second report[11] submitted a draft Bill which later formed the basis of the Adoption of Children Act 1926.

12. The 1926 Act applied only to England and Wales; a similar Act applicable to Scotland was passed in 1930. This legislation made legal adoption possible, but made no attempt to govern the activities of adoption societies. A Committee under the chairmanship of Miss Florence Horsbrugh MP was set up in 1936 to inquire into the methods of adoption societies and agencies and its report[12] resulted in the Adoption of Children (Regulation) Act 1939, which came into force in 1943. Further changes were made by the Adoption of Children Act 1949, and the former Adoption Acts were consolidated, with minor amendments, in the Adoption Act 1950.

13. Adoption law was last reviewed by the Hurst Committee, which reported in 1954.[8] The 1958 Act implemented most of the Hurst Committee's recommendations, and the three subsequent Adoption Acts have made no basic changes. The Adoption Act 1960 provides for the revocation of adoption orders in cases of legitimation, and the Adoption Act 1964 for the recognition of adoption orders made in the Isle of Man, the Channel Islands or Northern Ireland. The Adoption Act 1968 is concerned with international aspects of adoption, enabling courts to make orders under The Hague Convention on

the adoption of children,[13] and providing for the recognition of certain overseas adoption orders.

Adoption defined

14. Adoption means the complete severance of the legal relationship between parents and child and the establishment of a new one between the child and his adoptive parents. Although it is a formal legal procedure it deals with very human problems. It focusses primarily on the needs and well-being of individual children for whom this particular form of substitute care is considered appropriate. Nevertheless adoption has to be considered in a family context. It has important personal implications for several different sets of people: the natural and the adoptive parents, and their respective families, and the child himself. Parents, whether married or single, who are unable through adverse circumstances of one sort or another to bring up their child themselves in a stable family home can feel that in relinquishing their child they have secured for him a better future than they could offer. For some childless couples, adoption can satisfy the basic emotional need to create a family and to care for and rear children. It enables the child to achieve permanent security in a substitute home with a couple fully committed to fulfilling parental responsibilities. The child is the focal point in adoption; providing homes for children who need them is its primary purpose.

The need for adoption

15. The welfare of the child is best secured within his own family if he can be brought up in a stable and happy environment. If a child has no family this is obviously not possible, but where he has one parent the first step would seem to be to consider whether, with assistance where necessary, the parent can provide what the child needs for a secure and happy upbringing. The capacity of the parent to do this depends on a multiplicity of factors including her personality, the support available from family, friends and the community, the general attitude of society, and her material resources and prospects. In some cases, the provision of housing, financial assistance, day nursery care and other community services may enable a single parent to provide a satisfactory home for her child. We therefore welcomed the appointment by the Secretary of State for Social Services of a committee under the chairmanship of Mr Morris Finer QC to consider the needs of one-parent families. On the other hand, adoption may be desirable even where the child has two parents if they do not wish to bring up the child themselves or have little capacity for parenthood.

16. There are some children who cannot be brought up by their own parents, and society must offer a satisfactory alternative plan for the care and future development of such children. In some cases there is a strong bond with the wider natural family which should not be severed; in others the child's interests may best be served by the severance of such ties by means of adoption. The range of legal provisions relating to situations in which a child cannot be brought up by his own parents needs to be reviewed to ensure that it is comprehensive. We do this in Chapter 5. We are satisfied that there is a continuing need for adoption. It is one of a number of alternatives and is a satisfactory solution in many cases, but not in all.

4

The welfare of the child

17. In our working paper we said that the principle that the long-term welfare of the child should be the first and paramount consideration had influenced many of our propositions, both on the nature and extent of adoption services and on the resolution of conflicts. There was widespread support among our witnesses for this principle, which has been in the forefront of our minds when preparing our report and has influenced many of our recommendations.

18. We also suggested the application of this principle to adoption law. Here we had in mind the resolution of conflicts, because although the 1958 Act already requires the court to be satisfied that an adoption order, if made, will be for the welfare of the child, it does not contain a provision requiring the court, in cases where it is asked to dispense with the natural parents' consent, to consider the child's welfare at that stage. We think that the child's welfare should always be the first consideration. We consider in Chapter 8 the way in which this principle should be applied to the law on dispensing with consent to adoption.

The trend in adoption statistics

19. For ten years the number of adoptions registered in Great Britain rose steadily from 14,668 in 1958 to a peak of 26,986, and then declined (see Appendix B, Table 1 for statistics from 1927–1971). The provisional figure for the number of orders registered in 1971 is 23,399. The indications are that this downward trend is continuing. The figures include adoptions by natural parents, either alone or, much more commonly, with a step-parent. The number of these adoptions, particularly of legitimate children, has risen considerably in recent years and probably reflects the higher rates of divorce and remarriage. There were 10,849 such adoptions in 1970, an increase of 1,056 on the previous year, and they have continued to rise. (See Appendix B, Table 3). There has, therefore, been a sharper decline in the number of adoptions by non-relatives than in the number of adoptions overall.

20. This fall is the result of a smaller number of babies being offered for adoption, for there is no shortage of suitable couples wishing to adopt. The increasing number of legal abortions, more use of contraception, and the changing attitude to illegitimacy,* which has resulted in a higher proportion of unmarried mothers keeping their babies, are among the factors which may accentuate this trend. Unmarried mothers are gradually becoming less disadvantaged, and there is a significant increase in tolerance and understanding towards them and their children. Provisions to help them bring up their children have to some extent improved over the years. Supplementary benefit allowances, reasonable employment prospects and in some areas day care provision make the prospect of keeping a child more practicable.†

---

* For the numbers of illegitimate births see Appendix B, Table 5.

† The Church of England Board for Social Responsibility told us that in 1968 their Diocesan Moral and Social Welfare Councils were in contact with 19,493 mothers of children born illegitimate in that year, and of these 54·3 per cent decided to keep the child, and 34 per cent placed the child for adoption (2 per cent of the children were stillborn or died: other arrangements were made, or no decision had been taken, in respect of the remainder). The corresponding figures for 1971 were 13,165 mothers, of whom 65·0 per cent kept the child and 27·6 per cent placed the child for adoption.

21. However, children born out of wedlock, like children in other one-parent families, are often still badly disadvantaged. The Home Office, in the last report on the work of its Children's Department,[14] sounded a note of warning when it suggested that some of these unsupported mothers might subsequently find themselves unable to manage and ask the local authority to receive the child into care, or even place him for adoption. At this later stage a child's emotional development has often been adversely affected by a period of unstable care. A study made by the National Children's Bureau[15] of the social and educational effects of illegitimacy at birth and at seven years of age found that the difficulties experienced by the mothers were reflected in the abilities and attainments of their children. At the age of seven, these children had made less progress, on average, than legitimate children, while the highest performance was achieved by illegitimate children who were adopted. This was a cohort study and not a study in depth, and the results may be different if the children are followed to adolescence, but the evidence about seven-year-olds is a further reason why we welcome the current review of the needs of one-parent families.

Changing patterns in adoption

22. The recent trends in adoption have to be viewed against a complex background of altering values, as well as of rapid sociological change, which influence attitudes to illegitimacy, to infertility and to adoption. In view of the factors mentioned in paragraph 20 it is not surprising if the figures show a marked decline in the number of babies being offered for adoption. At the same time there are children with special needs who would benefit by adoption, but may not have been considered for it in the past when there were more babies available. As a result of medical advances more physically handicapped children now survive. It may be impracticable for an unsupported mother to bring up a handicapped child, but in the past some adoption agencies have been reluctant to consider such children for adoption placement. We are pleased to note that there is an increasing tendency for people to offer to bring up a handicapped child. Many such children could be adopted provided that the adopters fully understood and accepted the additional responsibility they were undertaking, and knew what supportive services were available to them. The increasing number of handicapped children now being considered for adoption reflects not only the higher survival rate, but also a determination that adoption should be available to all those who would benefit from it.

23. The difficulty of placing a coloured child for adoption was at one time so great, and so well known, that parents of those children rarely approached adoption agencies and the full extent of the need could not be estimated. The British Adoption Project established that, in 1966, 445 coloured children were adopted as a result of placement by adoption agencies, and that the agencies knew of 415 children whom they might have expected to place during that year but for their race. On the last day of that year 846 coloured children were on agencies' files as needing adoptive homes.[16] Since then the situation has improved, some agencies being able to place coloured children in their own areas without much difficulty, and others making use of the Adoption Resource Exchange, established by International Social Service, for inter-agency placements. The Adoption Resource Exchange placed 74 coloured children in 1971, but, while membership of the Exchange is expanding, it does

6

not yet cover the whole country. The Exchange is now finding homes for all the babies referred to it, and has extended its services to include older coloured children, but there are still reports from certain areas of parents who want their children adopted being told that there is little hope of placing a coloured child.[17]

24. Some children who would benefit from adoption have been handicapped by being past babyhood when they needed placement. There are obvious advantages in placing a child for adoption as young as possible, but recent research has shown that older children can be successfully adopted. Jaffee and Fanshel[18], in their follow-up study of 100 families in the New York area who had adopted children of three years of age or under in the period 1930–1940, found that

"in the main there was an absence of significant relationships between age at placement and adjustment in the various life-space areas we explored. The only area in which adjustment showed a significant association with placement age was that of the adoptees' social relationships. Contrary to expectations, the older the child had been upon coming into the adoptive home, the more positive was the description by his parents of his social adjustment over the years."

We share the authors' hope that their findings will encourage those who have been hesitant to promote the adoption of children who are no longer babies, but are in early childhood, at least to reconsider the basis for this reluctance. We believe that adoption should be one of the alternatives to be considered when an older child needs a permanent substitute home. Among these children will be some born with physical handicaps who have been in hospital for a lengthy period (see paragraph 22). The findings of Dr Hilda Lewis[19] and Alfred Kadushin[20] also encourage us to think that older children can be successfully adopted, although this does not detract from the principle that, in general, adoption placements are best made at an early age.

25. Other children have been handicapped by their family histories and have not been considered for adoption for this reason. Advances in knowledge indicate that some adverse factors in parental histories, e.g. criminality, promiscuity, or certain types of mental illness and mental subnormality, may have no genetic relevance to the future development of a child, and therefore adoption should not be eliminated on such grounds alone when considering the alternatives available. Even where agencies have taken professional advice, and established that a particular family history is irrelevant to the child's development, we have been told that sometimes they have been reluctant to place children for adoption because of uncertainty about the attitude of the courts, and the risk that the court will cause anxiety to the adopters by giving them irrelevant adverse information of this sort about the natural parents. It is often these children who most need to have the security which adoption can give, and we hope that courts will bear this in mind.

26. The Association of British Adoption Agencies is currently conducting a study of children needing permanent substitute parents. The aim is to find out whether or not there are children in the care of local authorities and voluntary societies for whom adoption would be the plan of choice and, if

so, what is preventing their placement. The findings of this study should be available early in 1973 and should provide valuable information as to whether there is, as some suspect, a considerable number of older children in care whose need for adoption is not being met.

27. While adoption agencies may in future consider the placement of children with more varied needs, those coming forward as adopters may also be from a broader cross-section of the community. While there are still many childless couples seeking to adopt, it seems possible that greater medical knowledge and skill in the field of infertility may help to reduce their numbers. At the same time couples who would like a larger family may decide that, rather than have another child of their own, they would like to offer a permanent home to a child in need of one. There is increased consciousness of the positive benefits such families have to offer an adopted child; in some cases their experience with their own children enables them to cope with a child with some special need more easily than could a couple without previous experience of parenthood.

28. Side by side with these changes there are developments in our understanding of the needs of adopted children as they grow up. There is growing acceptance that bringing up children by adoption is different from bringing up natural children. The difference springs basically from the fact that adoptive parents need to be good parents to someone else's child.* The importance of telling a child that he is adopted has long been recognised, and there is growing recognition that the child should be told early and helped to understand it more fully as he grows older. It is also increasingly recognised that at some stage the child will need to know about his origins—the positive factors about his parents, such as any special qualities, gifts or interests; their appearance; their reason for giving him up; and any medical background which may be relevant. This kind of information helps the proper development of a sense of identity, and gives the child and his adoptive parents a fuller understanding of him as an individual with his own unique combination of characteristics, both inherited and acquired from his upbringing and environment. Adopters must therefore be provided with relevant background information and agencies must see that help is readily available if the adopters need advice on how best to convey this information to the child. We discuss the question of access to original birth records in Chapter 11.

29. Sharing of relevant information about natural parents is not easily reconciled with some aspects of the concept of adoption as a completely new start. Attitudes to adoption are, however, changing in line with more openness about family and social matters and we think that more honesty about the adoptive status is to be encouraged.

Recommendation
30. We conclude that there is a continuing need for adoption, by which we mean the permanent legal transfer of parental rights and responsibilities, although there are changes in the patterns of adoption, with fewer healthy babies and more children with special needs requiring placement, and there

---

* A Guide to Adoption Practice[3] paragraph III, 40.

is a need for greater understanding, among agencies and courts, of the possibility of successful adoption of children with special needs. We accordingly *recommend* that:—

The law should continue to provide for the adoption of children.

(Recommendation 1)

CHAPTER 3

PROVISION OF AN ADOPTION SERVICE

31. The continuing need for adoption implies a need for social work services for all those concerned: natural parents, prospective adopters and, above all, the children. These services cannot be considered satisfactory if the level of provision varies in quality and quantity in different parts of the country.

The present situation

32. There are 63 voluntary adoption societies in England and Wales and 8 in Scotland. Geographically the development of the societies has been uneven. Some societies serve a local area, others operate nationally. Some offer a range of child care and family services, while others deal only with the selection of adoptive homes and the placement of children. Some societies restrict their services to certain groups of people. In other cases, a lack of trained social work staff or of a range of resources imposes restrictions on the service offered; for example, agencies without foster home or nursery provision may be unable to accept children with special needs. Only a few voluntary societies have the resources to offer continuing help to mothers who keep their children.

33. Ninety-six of the 172 local authorities in England and Wales act as adoption agencies and the number is slowly increasing. All 52 authorities in Scotland except one have placed children for adoption in recent years, though the involvement of some of the smaller authorities is fairly infrequent and may occur simply as a result of some existing concern with the child. Over Great Britain as a whole, local authorities have made no systematic attempt to assess the needs of their areas and to develop services accordingly, and we have been told of areas which are ill-served. Moreover, where local authorities do provide a service, not all have integrated their adoption work with their other services for children and families.

34. These factors influence considerably the kinds of people, whether children, natural parents or prospective adopters, to whom a service is available and the quality of the service which is offered. What is needed is a service which is comprehensive in scope and available throughout the country.

The objectives and organisation
of a comprehensive service

35. The service must meet the needs of children, persons wishing to adopt and natural parents. Local authority social services departments and voluntary organisations with a range of services for children should be able to offer a better and more comprehensive service for children than purely placement agencies, since they have a wider range of resources. This is particularly important where children with special needs are concerned (see paragraph 22), where more time is needed to find suitable homes, as well as good assessment facilities and highly developed casework skills.

36. If adoption is a child-centred service, aimed at providing homes for children, the service which an agency will offer to couples wishing to adopt will be ancillary to this central aim. Few adoption societies are likely at the present time to be able to use their scarce resources to offer a social work service to childless couples where there is little prospect of accepting them as applicants and placing a child with them, but such couples may need help in coming to terms with their disappointment.

37. Consideration of the service which should be given to natural parents brings out the need to define where the boundaries of an adoption service lie. Many witnesses said that some of the pressure on an unmarried mother to place her child for adoption arose out of inadequate housing and financial resources. Yet it is unrealistic to suppose that an adoption service could itself attempt to provide for these needs. We have referred in paragraph 15 to the consideration by the Finer Committee of the problems facing one-parent families in general. A good adoption service should, however, have links with the departments of local and central government (such as housing departments and the Department of Health and Social Security) which provide general services to the community at large, and with voluntary agencies and self-help groups concerned with one-parent families.

38. What then should a comprehensive service cover? We consider that it should comprise a social work service to natural parents, whether married or unmarried, seeking placement for a child (which would include channels of communication with related community resources); skills and facilities for the assessment of the parents' emotional resources, and their personal and social situation; short-term accommodation for unsupported mothers; general child care resources, including short-term placement facilities for children pending adoption placement; assessment facilities; adoption placement services; after-care for natural parents who need it; counselling for adoptive families. In addition, it should have access to a range of specialised services, such as medical services (including genetic, psychiatric and psychological assessment services, arrangements for the examination of children and adoptive applic-ants, and a medical adviser) and legal advisory services. The kind of service we have in mind is described fully in A Guide to Adoption Practice.[3]

39. It follows from this that, if agencies which are not purely placement agencies are to continue, they will need to expand in order to provide a range of options, continuity of casework and access to general child care resources. This may involve, in the short term, their making formal arrangements for a sharing of resources with local authorities or general child care agencies, while aiming in the long term to offer a more extended service themselves. Where adoption is one of the functions of a general family social work agency, it should be related to other parts of the agency's work, with good com-munication and co-ordination between the various groups of workers and services.

40. As well as being comprehensive in scope, the service should be available in all parts of the country. We referred in our working paper to "a nation-wide comprehensive service". Some of our witnesses understood us to be suggesting a single national adoption service as a long-term aim. This was not our intention

and the great majority of our witnesses were opposed to this concept. What we have in mind is the development of professional services available to children, natural parents and adopters regardless of where they happen to live or of their racial or religious background.

41. We see a continuing place for the voluntary societies in the adoption field. They have been the pioneers of adoption, have promoted and developed knowledge and skills; and they provide a choice of service. Quite apart from the principle that voluntary organisations have a part to play in the provision of adoption services, the resources and skills of the voluntary societies will continue to be indispensable for the foreseeable future. In 1971, voluntary societies placed about 5,650 children for adoption compared with about 4,130 placed by local authorities.*

42. In order to ensure the provision of a service of the kind we have described, available to all those needing it in any part of the country, we propose that new reponsibilities should be placed on local authorities. In the first place, local authorities should have a statutory duty to provide an adoption service as part of their general child care and family casework provision. A local authority social service cannot be considered comprehensive if adoption is not included. In the second place, it should be the duty of the local authority to ensure that a comprehensive service is available throughout their area. This will require an assessment, in co-operation with voluntary societies, of the needs of the area and of the resources available to meet them, and a co-ordinated plan for the provision of the service. In setting up their own service, the authority would take into account the services provided by voluntary agencies.

43. The recommendations which we have made in paragraphs 38 and 39 may result in some voluntary societies increasing in size, and in other cases will tend to promote mergers, while the reorganisation of local government will create larger local authorities. These changes need not supplant the kinds of development now taking place, such as groupings of agencies, pairing arrangements and other forms of co-operation. We consider that there should be a phasing out of those voluntary adoption societies which are unable or unwilling to provide a comprehensive service, and the recommendations on registration which we make later in this chapter are designed to have that effect.

Recommendations

44. An adoption service should be available throughout the country, for children, natural parents and persons wishing to adopt, focussing primarily on the needs of children. It should be part of a comprehensive social work service for children and families. There is a continuing place and need for voluntary effort in adoption. Accordingly *we recommend* that:—

> The law should place on local authorities a duty to provide an adoption service as part of their general child care and family casework provision.
> (Recommendation 2)

---

* See Appendix B, Table 4. Precise figures for local authority placements are not available because the figures for children in care who are adopted do not distinguish between children placed directly for adoption and children who are boarded out with foster parents and eventually adopted by them.

Local authorities should have a statutory duty to ensure, in co-operation with voluntary societies, that a comprehensive adoption service is available throughout their area.

(Recommendation 3)

Ensuring and developing standards

45. Many of our recommendations have been made on the assumption that adoption agency practice will be of a good standard; indeed they will depend upon this for their success. More trained social workers are required, but this, and the reorganisation of adoption services, will not of themselves be sufficient to secure adequate and developing standards of practice. This requires the application of systematised knowledge and research; a range of promotional activities such as training, conferences, seminars and literature; and the ready availability to local authorities and voluntary societies alike of the advice and guidance of central government professional services. A more effective system for the registration of voluntary societies is also required.

Central advice and guidance

46. The central government professional services in this field now consist of the Social Work Service in England and Wales and the Central Advisory Service of the Social Work Services Group in Scotland. These operate as advisory and consultancy services across the whole field of the social services functions (in Scotland, the social work functions) of local authorities, including adoption, and have certain statutory powers of inspection. They offer help and guidance to local authorities and voluntary organisations on professional practice and standards designed to further developments which enhance the quality of service. They participate in the promotional activities mentioned in paragraph 45 and in the spreading of knowledge arising from these activities.*

47. These services have a significant contribution to make in the promotion of standards, and clearly they should be as freely available, in the adoption field, to local authorities and voluntary adoption societies alike, as in other areas of social work practice. The services should, if necessary, be strengthened to allow for this. The role of the central government service must, however, be seen as complementary to, and parallel with, the increasing trend among local authorities to assume responsibility themselves for quality control in the services which they provide.

Registration of voluntary societies

48. A voluntary social work agency is not publicly accountable for its work in the same way as a statutory body. In the absence of this public accountability, arrangements must be made to ensure its capacity to undertake this kind of work. At present these arrangements take the form of a legal requirement that voluntary adoption societies must register with the local authority in whose area their administrative centre is situated. Registration

---

* At present officers authorised by the Secretary of State have power to enter and inspect premises in which children are accommodated, e.g. children's homes (whether local authority or voluntary) and foster homes. There is no other power to inspect voluntary organisations or societies, e.g. to inspect their organisational system or their records. Advice and guidance is given on an informal basis. Local authorities have access to the books and records of adoption societies for the purpose of deciding whether a registration should be cancelled.

13

amounts to the grant of a licence to operate, and we think the principle of requiring registration of voluntary societies is right.

49. Under the present law (section 30 of the 1958 Act) the registration of a voluntary adoption society must be refused if the local authority is not satisfied that it is a charitable organisation and may be refused on any one of three grounds.

(1) The activities of the society are not controlled by a committee of its members responsible to its members.

(2) A person employed for adoption purposes is not a fit or proper person, or any person taking part in the management or control of the society or any member of the society has been convicted of one of a number of specified offences connected with adoption.

(3) The number of competent staff employed by the society is insufficient having regard to the extent of its activities.

Registration may be cancelled on any ground which would have entitled the local authority to refuse registration, and the authority has power (section 33 of the 1958 Act) to call for information about the society's work which is relevant to the exercise of this power. Appeal against a refusal to register or a cancellation of registration lies to the Crown Court in England and Wales and to the sheriff court in Scotland.

50. We think that these powers could have been more effectively used but, even so, the criteria for registration and the grounds for refusing and cancelling registration are too narrow. In our working paper we suggested that the criteria should be extended so as to ensure that each voluntary agency, through its own resources or in conjunction with other agencies, could make an effective contribution towards a comprehensive service. We set out in broad terms the kind of criteria which would be considered by the registering authority and suggested that agencies should be required to provide information relating to these criteria when applying for registration. We suggested that registration should be renewable every three years. There was almost unanimous agreement with these suggestions.

The registering authority

51. The way in which a new registration system would operate depends to some extent on who would be the registering authority. In our working paper we invited comments on whether this should be central or local government. We set out the arguments, which may be summarised as follows.

Arguments in favour of central registration

(a) Local registration inhibits good relationships between a local authority and a voluntary adoption society, introducing an authoritative element in what should be a partnership between statutory and voluntary bodies.

(b) Local authorities have difficulty in demanding standards from voluntary organisations which they are not always able to match in their own services because of a shortage of skilled and experienced social workers.

(c) The existing registration by local authorities has failed to achieve adequate standards.

14

(d) Some local authorities are too small effectively to register a large national or regional society whose headquarters happen to be situated in their area.

(e) Only central registration could achieve uniformly good standards of practice throughout the country.

Arguments in favour of local registration

(a) Local authorities have a much more intimate knowledge of the needs and resources of the area than central government can have, and will have an even greater knowledge when they are responsible for ensuring the provision of a comprehensive service throughout the area.

(b) Local authorities will in future be larger and stronger and, given strengthened criteria for registration, with guidance on the methods of carrying it out, they should be well able to become effective registering authorities.

(c) The general trend in government is for responsibility for quality control to be assumed by local authorities themselves. Indeed, in Scotland, no other comparable service is now subject to central registration.

52. The majority of our witnesses were in favour of registration by central government. Local authorities and voluntary societies alike have urged this upon us. There was a strong body of opinion which considered that registration should be linked with inspection by the central government's professional social work advisers. The central government professional services now function as advisory and consultancy services across the whole field of social work (see paragraph 46), and the character of central oversight has changed. We were advised that it is no longer desirable in principle, or practicable on staffing grounds, to retain detailed inspection of adoption, which is only a small section of this wide field. There is thus the possibility that central registration could become a matter of remote administrative decision, all too easily divorced from a detailed first-hand knowledge of the agency concerned.

53. A number of compromise suggestions were put forward. One was that registration should rest initially with central government and later be transferred to local authorities. Another was that registration should be a joint exercise, the central government taking the decision after obtaining a report from the local authority. We think that compromises that confuse accountability might produce the worst of both worlds.

54. We have decided in favour of central government registration. The arguments which have weighed most with us are the urgent need to ensure good standards throughout the country, which we think will be more effectively achieved by central registration, and to ensure a partnership between local authorities and voluntary societies in planning a comprehensive adoption service. Such a partnership will be easier to build if one partner is not responsible for registering the other.

55. Some of our witnesses suggested that if central government were the registering body, local authorities should also have to seek registration. This would be inconsistent with our recommendation that local authorities should

have a duty to provide an adoption service. The criteria for registration would, however, provide guidelines to local authorities and to the central government advisory services when reviewing local authority practice.

Registration machinery

56. We consider that the Secretary of State should be empowered to register a voluntary society only if he is satisfied that the proposed scope of the society's activities, the nature of its resources and the effectiveness of its organisation are such that the society is likely to make an effective contribution towards a comprehensive adoption service in the area in which it proposes to operate.

57. We do not consider ourselves competent to suggest to the central government departments precisely how the scrutiny of agencies should be carried out. We envisage that, in the first instance, an agency applying for registration should be required to furnish the Secretary of State with written information. We set out in Appendix C the kind of information which we think might be required, although this is a matter on which the Secretary of State might wish to consult the Personal Social Services Council.*

58. Having obtained this information, we think that the central government department should satisfy itself about the following matters.
 (a) *The agency's programme.* The department should examine the information about the nature, scope, size and geographical area of the programme and satisfy itself that the programme would make an effective contribution towards a comprehensive service.
 (b) *The agency's resources.* The department should examine the information about the agency's resources for carrying out the programme, including its own resources, resources available to it by arrangement with other agencies and services, staff of all kinds and their qualifications, medical resources, access to other consultancy services and financial resources, and satisfy itself that these resources are adequate to carry out effectively the agency's programme.
 (c) *The agency's organisation.* The department should examine the information on the agency's organisation, including staff responsibilities and relationships, and decision-making and consultative machinery, and satisfy itself that the organisation is appropriate for the effective carrying out of the programme.

59. Registration should be renewable every three years and societies would be required to furnish the same information as is required on initial registration. We recommend that the Secretary of State should have power, as local authorities now have, to cancel registration at any time; the power given to local authorities, by section 33 of the 1958 Act, to call for information relevant to the power to cancel registration, should be transferred to the Secretary of State.

60. The present system of appeal to a court against refusal of registration,

---

* In Scotland, the Advisory Council on Social Work.

16

or a cancellation of registration, is not inappropriate to the existing narrow factual criteria. The new criteria we have recommended involve an assessment of the general competence and effectiveness of an agency rather than the establishment of matters of fact, and it is not, in our view, appropriate for appeals against refusal or cancellation of registration to lie to a court. We have considered whether there should be an appeal to some specially constituted tribunal, but, on balance, bearing in mind that the Secretary of State is answerable to Parliament for his decisions, we think that special appeal machinery is unnecessary.

Recommendations

61. The existing system of registering voluntary adoption societies is ineffective and the criteria are too narrow. Broader criteria should be laid down and registration by the central government would be the most effective way of ensuring good standards throughout the country. Accordingly *we recommend* that:—

The central government professional advisory and consultancy services should be available to all voluntary adoption societies.

(Recommendation 4)

Responsibility for registering voluntary adoption societies should rest with the Secretary of State.

(Recommendation 5)

Registration should be renewable every three years.

(Recommendation 6)

The Secretary of State should have power to call for information and to cancel registration.

(Recommendation 7)

Criteria should be prescribed which are relevant to the programme, resources and organisation of voluntary societies.

(Recommendation 8)

The financing of the adoption service

62. Lack of money may inhibit improvement in agency standards. In particular, if voluntary societies are to continue to play an important role in adoption they will need to be adequately financed. Three sources of money are open to them: fund raising (including donations by adopters); fees or expenses charged to adopters; and grants from local authorities.

63. Section 50(3) of the 1958 Act allows agencies to charge "expenses reasonably incurred . . . in connection with the adoption of the infant". There is therefore no statutory obligation on either voluntary agencies or local authorities to provide a free service and no legal prohibition on the charging of expenses. Local authorities in England and Wales have power under section 46(2) of the Children Act 1948 to make contributions to voluntary organisations whose object is to promote the welfare of children and, although this covers grants for adoption work, in practice only small grants are made. Section 10(3) of the Social Work (Scotland) Act 1968 empowers local authorities to make contributions to voluntary organisations which are concerned with the promotion of social welfare. We understand that this power has not been widely used to make substantial grants to voluntary adoption societies.

64. The evidence we received expressed a wide variety of opinions on the practice of charging fees or expenses or seeking donations from adopters. Some witnesses thought that this transferred the emphasis from the child to the adopter and that it was inconsistent with the increased attention being given to finding homes for children with special needs. Yet most voluntary societies cannot afford to give up these sources of income unless others are found.

65. We see no objection in principle to the charging of expenses, and recognise that donations by adopters form an essential part of the income of some voluntary societies. Many adopters are able and ready to pay some or all of the expenses incurred by the agency. On the other hand we think it would be wrong to require expenses to be charged. We prefer the present situation which allows flexibility.

66. In our working paper we suggested that, in so far as voluntary societies make an essential contribution to the provision of adoption services in their areas, local authorities should recognise their work by giving realistic financial support based on actual costs.* There was wide support for this suggestion among our witnesses and it was argued that in many cases societies provided a service which would otherwise fall to the authority itself. We think that a proper assessment of reasonable costs in adoption work should become an established practice both of local authorities and voluntary societies and that local authorities, as part of their responsibility to ensure the provision of a comprehensive service in their area, should make realistic financial arrangements with voluntary societies participating in that service.

Recommendations

67. Agencies should remain free to charge expenses and to accept contributions towards the cost of arranging adoptions.

(Recommendation 9)

Local authorities should make realistic financial arrangements with voluntary adoption societies participating in the provision of the adoption service in their areas and make contributions towards the work of the societies which bear some relation to the actual costs incurred.

(Recommendation 10)

Timing of the changes

68. We envisage that the Secretary of State will give the voluntary societies notice of the date on which the changes in registration law will come into effect, and by which societies will have to be registered under the new procedure if they are to continue to arrange adoptions. This will be necessary in order that societies can prepare themselves to fulfil the new registration criteria. At the same time societies should be told what information they will be required to supply when applying for registration. Societies will need time to reach these new standards.

---

* The need for more financial help to voluntary adoption societies by local authorities was stressed in the Hurst Report[8]. (Paragraph 40.)

69. Some of the recommendations which we make later in this report are not intended to be brought into operation until societies have been registered under the new machinery which we have recommended. We identify these recommendations in the relevant parts of our report.

CHAPTER 4

ADOPTION: ELIGIBILITY OF ADOPTERS, WHO MAY ARRANGE IT AND SHOULD IT BE SUBSIDISED

Legal criteria for eligibility to adopt

70. The crucial decision in the adoption process is the decision about the placement of the child. Not only the professional competence of the placement agency but, equally, its criteria for the selection of adoptive applicants are of first importance. The question is how far these criteria should be prescribed by law.

71. The criteria in the existing law relate to domicile, residence, marital status and minimum age. Subject to these few statutory requirements, decisions on the suitability of adopters are left to the judgment of agencies and the courts, although there are statutory rules and regulations which lay down in considerable detail the factual information about adoptive applicants which must be obtained by the agency and the guardian ad litem, and which must be given by the adopters in their form of application to the court.

72. We are satisfied that detailed criteria of suitability cannot be prescribed by statute, and that this must continue to be left to the judgment of agencies and courts. Besides obtaining factual information an agency will explore the attitudes and motives of applicants and assess their personal qualities and, for example, the significance of any age gap between husband and wife, the stability of the employment record, and the adequacy of the housing. A Guide to Adoption Practice,[3] Chapter III, lists the many aspects of a couple's attitude to life which should be taken into consideration.

73. Some agencies have their own criteria, possibly imposed by the terms of their constitution. For example, they may confine their service largely to persons of a particular religious denomination. We consider that voluntary societies should have the right to cater for certain sections of the community if they wish, provided that they fulfil the criteria for registration. Agencies with long waiting lists may sometimes be unable to consider further applicants. We deprecate, however, arbitrary criteria such as the exclusion of couples with children of their own, or refusing to accept for adoption a mother's second and subsequent illegitimate children. We have been given examples of arbitrary rules of this kind being followed by agencies and courts. We think that each case should be considered on its merits, from the point of view of whether adoption is likely to be for the child's welfare, and that agencies and courts should not themselves attempt to formulate rigid rules on what constitutes suitability, or unsuitability, to adopt.

74. In the light of our conclusion that suitability must be assessed in each individual case, what criteria for eligibility should be laid down by law? It is clear that certain basic conditions of eligibility to adopt should be

defined by statute, and we recommend no change in the requirements regarding domicile, residence and marital status.

75. We suggested in our working paper that any adult who fulfilled these conditions should be legally eligible to adopt. This would have meant abandoning any minimum age for adoption. The minimum age is at present 25 years for a sole adopter unrelated to the child, while in the case of a married couple one must be aged at least 25 and the other at least 21. For adoption by a natural parent, whether alone or jointly with her spouse, there is no minimum age, but other relatives must be aged at least 21 years.

76. Our suggestion had a mixed reception. A number of witnesses expressed concern about the high incidence of breakdown of young marriages and suggested that either a minimum age or a minimum length of marriage should be stipulated. We agree that the stability of the marriage is an important factor and may be difficult to assess until the marriage has subsisted for some time. We do not, however, wish to hamper professional judgment by recommending a minimum period because circumstances vary greatly.

77. We have received evidence that the existing minimum age of 25 for one of the spouses has prevented some suitable couples from being considered, and we think that the age should be lowered. We accept, however, that 18 is a young age at which to face up to all the implications of taking responsibility for someone else's child. A minimum age of 21 would ensure that the teenage marriages which appear to be more vulnerable would have been tested by time.* We therefore recommend that a minimum age for adopters should be retained, and that it should be the age of 21 for both husband and wife in all cases.

78. Section 2(3) of the 1958 Act prohibits the adoption of a female by a sole male applicant unless the court is satisfied that there are special circumstances† which justify as an exceptional measure the making of an adoption order. We see no need to retain this prohibition. The court is required by section 7(b) of the 1958 Act to be satisfied in every case that the adoption order, if made, will be for the welfare of the child, and we see no reason to single out this one set of circumstances where adoption will rarely be for the welfare of the child.

79. We do not consider that there is any need to continue to prescribe in regulations the information which agencies should collect about prospective adopters. Some of the information now prescribed is necessary in any event to determine whether the adopters fulfil the requirements of section 1 of the 1958 Act. It is not practicable to lay down in regulations all the other information required to enable the agency to judge the suitability of the applicants; this should be left to the agencies. We see the information which

---

* Of the teenage girls marrying in 1960, approximately 9 per cent had become divorced by the end of 1969, whereas the divorce rate for all marriages in 1960 was just under 5 per cent by the end of 1969.[21]

† The applicant may, for example, be the girl's putative father; in 1970 2 putative fathers were successful sole applicants for adoption orders in respect of their illegitimate daughters (see paragraph 99).

agencies should normally collect about applicants as a matter for guidance rather than legal prescription. A prescribed form for applying to a court for an adoption order, covering the basic information required by the court, will continue to be required.

Recommendations

80. *We recommend* that:—
The basic legal conditions of eligibility to adopt a child should cover the domicile, residence, minimum age and marital status of the adopters. The minimum age should be 21 years. The prohibition in section 2(3) of the 1958 Act should be repealed.

(Recommendation 11)

The information which agencies should obtain about prospective adopters should no longer be prescribed by law.

(Recommendation 12)

Who may arrange adoptions

81. Most adoptions by non-relatives are arranged through an adoption agency. But the law also allows adoptions which are not arranged through agencies. These are known as "independent adoptions". Most of them are adoptions by relatives, but there is a small number of adoptions by strangers in which an agency plays no part. Sometimes the arrangements are made direct between the natural parent and the adopters; these are known as "direct placements"; sometimes they are made by a private person, who may be, for instance, a friend, the family doctor or a solicitor, or a person who makes a regular practice of arranging adoptions, or even a casual acquaintance, such as someone the mother meets in a launderette. A private individual who arranges an adoption is known as a "third party".

82. The statistical survey carried out in 1966[1] covered a sample of some 3,400 adoption applications made in that year to 138 courts in Great Britain. These adoptions were arranged as follows:

	Per Cent	Per Cent
Adoptions arranged by voluntary societies ..	40	
Adoptions arranged by local authorities	19	
Total of agency adoptions		59
Adoptions by parents	29	
Direct placements with relatives	5	
Direct placements with non-relatives	3	
Adoptions arranged by third parties	4	
Total of independent adoptions		41
		100

83. The Hurst Committee[8] estimated that in 1954 more than one-third of non-relative adoptions resulted from placements by third parties or by the natural parents. The 1966 survey figures given above show that the proportion was then very much less. Nevertheless there were some 1,500 children a year

22

placed in this way. There are a number of reasons why people make independent arrangements without using agency services. One is the inaccessibility of agencies in some areas, which our recommendations in Chapter 3 are designed to remedy. Others are people's dislike of the idea of enquiries by an agency, a desire to keep control of the situation themselves, or their trust in a person known to them, such as their family doctor. Some would-be adopters have been turned down by agencies, and others may seek independent placements because they realise that no adoption agency would consider them suitable.

84. Much concern has been expressed about these placements. The decision to place a child with a particular couple is the most important stage in the adoption process. Adoption law must give assurance of adequate safeguards for the welfare of the child at this stage, otherwise it is ineffective. This assurance rests mainly upon the skilled work of the adoption services, which includes preparation for adoptive parenthood. An independent adoption is one in which this assurance is lacking. We therefore suggested in our working paper that independent placements with non-relatives should no longer be allowed.

85. The evidence we received was divided. The main arguments against our proposal were that it was an interference with individual liberty, particularly in the case of direct placements by the mother; that there was no research evidence to prove that independent placements were any worse than agency placements, and that they should not be banned until agency work had improved; and that the investigation by the guardian ad litem and a court hearing were sufficient safeguards against adoption orders being made in respect of unsuitable placements. We were more convinced by the contrary arguments, and many witnesses agreed with our reasoning and expressed strong support for our suggestion.

86. Virtually no recent research has been done to compare the outcome of independent placements with that of agency placements, but there is no lack of evidence of unsatisfactory independent placements. Information received from the Church of England Board for Social Responsibility, which has contact with agencies working with unmarried mothers, revealed that in the course of a year a considerable number of highly unsatisfactory independent placements came to the notice of the social workers. Local authorities with experience of acting as guardians ad litem or carrying out welfare supervision of children placed for adoption have come across unsatisfactory independent placements which would not have been made by a reputable adoption agency. This is confirmed by the written and oral evidence we have received and by the personal experience of some of our members.

87. The statistical survey of adoption in Great Britain[1] showed that 31 per cent of third party placements were made by doctors or by the matrons of nursing homes where the child was born. Although the survey covered a sample of only about one-seventh of adoption applications made in 1966, one consultant at a private clinic was responsible for six placements within the sample, and five of the seven nursing home

matrons had made more than one placement.* It is therefore of interest that there was considerable support from the medical professional associations for banning independent placements, the British Medical Association urging that the proposal should be implemented as soon as possible. The greater imbalance between the numbers of couples wishing to adopt and the number of babies needing adoption could lead to an increase in third party activity in future. We have received no direct evidence of financial transactions in third party placements, but it is within the knowledge of some of our members that couples have alleged that they have paid an inflated fee for the investigation of infertility on the understanding that a child would be found for them to adopt, and that mothers have alleged that services, such as nursing home facilities, have been provided on the understanding that the child would be available for adoption.

88. Adoption is a matter of such vital importance to a child (who is usually too young to have any say in the matter) that society has a duty to ensure that the most satisfactory placements are made. Society manifestly does not do so while it is open to anybody to place a child for adoption. While the court hearing is intended as a final safeguard, safeguards are needed much earlier. Moreover courts are in difficulty about refusing to make an adoption order because there is no agency to which the child can be returned. Adoption agencies are increasingly staffed by social workers whose professional skills and knowledge are increasing. Agency practice has built-in safeguards through the Adoption Agencies Regulations and through general accountability to the public. We therefore adhere to the view expressed in our working paper that independent placements should not be allowed once the new registration system for adoption agencies is in force, when these safeguards will be even greater. We include in this proposal direct placements by the parents, although, if they wished a particular placement to be made, the agency arranging the adoption should give this sympathetic consideration.

89. We turn now to the way in which our proposal should be implemented. We are aware of the fear of the Hurst Committee[8] that a ban on independent placements would lead to evasion and we have therefore considered with some care the practical implications of a ban.

90. In the first place, we think it should be an offence for a person other than an adoption agency to place a child for adoption. It has been put to us that Parliament might be reluctant to make it a criminal offence for a mother to place her own child. Nevertheless, in our view, the making of adoption placements by any persons other than agencies must be prohibited if the welfare of children is to be properly safeguarded. In addition, it should be an offence to receive a child for adoption otherwise than through an adoption agency registered in this country. This would provide a safeguard

---

* It is estimated that 6 individuals were in 1966 responsible for between 10 and 50 placements each; one who made 7 placements within the sample studied was subsequently instrumental in forming a new voluntary society, which has been registered as an adoption agency; another who made three placements within the sample was a private foster mother who was said to have made "many placings in various parts of the country. Her unorthodox methods have been criticised by county court judges but no evidence of financial transactions is available".[1] About half the third party placements in 1966 were thought to have been by friends, relatives or chance acquaintances of the parents who were unlikely to have acted in this way more than once.

24

for children from abroad placed with couples in this country either through private arrangements or through foreign organisations (see paragraphs 322 to 325).

91. We realise the limitations of the criminal law in this field, and in particular the difficulty of proving that a placement was for the express purpose of adoption and not for other purposes, e.g. temporary care by foster parents. The prohibition we propose would not mean that parents would cease to be able to arrange for the care of their child by others. It might be possible, therefore, to evade the prohibition by a placement, ostensibly for fostering, followed by an application to adopt. In our working paper we suggested meeting this possibility by prohibiting adoptions by foster parents unless they had cared for the child for at least twelve months. The majority of witnesses were opposed to this suggestion on the ground that children are often placed with foster parents by local authorities and adoption societies with the possibility of adoption in mind, but not, at that stage, expressly for the purpose of adoption. We think our original purpose would be met if it were provided that the period should be twelve months except where the child was placed with foster parents by an adoption agency and we recommend accordingly.

Recommendations

92. Independent placements should not be allowed once the new registration procedure has come into force. To achieve this *we recommend* that:—

The law should make it an offence for a person other than an adoption agency to place a child with a person who is not a relative (as defined in the 1958 Act) for the purpose of adoption.

(Recommendation 13)

The law should make it an offence for a person who is not a relative (as defined in the 1958 Act) to receive a child for the purpose of adoption otherwise than through an adoption agency registered in this country.

(Recommendation 14)

The law should require an applicant for an adoption order, who is not a relative, to have cared for the child for twelve months or more if the child was not placed with him by an adoption agency.

(Recommendation 15)

These provisions should be brought into effect once the new registration system is in force and agencies are registered under the new system.

(Recommendation 16)

Should adoption be subsidised?

93. We suggested in our working paper that consideration should be given to the possibility of guardians and adopters being paid regular subsidies in appropriate cases, and we said that we would welcome views on this. While there was considerable support for allowances for guardians (see Chapter 6), many witnesses saw a clear distinction between adoption and guardianship and opposed the idea of any payments to adopters. Some took the view that payment would conflict with the principle that adoption should put the child in precisely the same position as a child born to the adopters. While some agreed with our suggestion that, if allowances were payable, more homes might be found for children with special needs, others said that it would be

unfair to the parents of handicapped children if the adopters of these children could get an allowance which was not available to their natural parents. Some said that the law should not forbid agency payments to adopters but that there should be no national system of allowances.

94. We recognise the objection to singling out handicapped adopted children for special payments, and we do not advocate payments for adopters generally. However, we still think that there is a case for allowances in some circumstances, for example, where suitable adopters are available for a family of children who need to be kept together but, for financial reasons, adoption is not possible if an allowance cannot be paid. Although most witnesses were opposed to our suggestion, we should like to see a period of experiment during which evidence could be gathered. But at present even experiment is not possible, because it would contravene the law, and we recommend that the law should be amended so as to enable payments to be made by a few charitable bodies specially authorised by the Secretary of State for this purpose. There may be a number of difficulties, and we suggest pilot schemes which could be reviewed after, say, seven years, although the subsidy would have to be continued to those who had adopted on that basis for as long as they needed it.

Recommendation

95. *We recommend* that:—

The law should be amended to permit pilot schemes of payment of allowances to adopters under the general oversight of the Secretary of State.

(Recommendation 17)

CHAPTER 5

RELATIVES—ADOPTION OR GUARDIANSHIP?

96. The present law permits adoptions by those who are related to a child by blood or marriage. These include many adoptions by natural parents and step-parents.

97. "A Survey of Adoption in Great Britain"[1] showed that, in 1966, 66 per cent of adoptions were by non-relatives, 29 per cent by parents (mainly natural parent and step-parent, but in a few cases a natural parent alone) and 5 per cent by other relatives. Since then the number of adoptions by parents and step-parents has increased and there is reason to think that this is a continuing trend. This latter category differs fundamentally from adoptions by non-relatives, which create relationships where previously there were none. Adoption by relatives* severs in law, but not in fact, an existing relationship of blood or of affinity, and creates an adoptive relationship in place of the natural relationship which in fact, though not in law, continues unchanged. In most cases the adopting relatives are already caring for the child and will continue to do so whether or not they adopt him; and adoption by relatives can be particularly harmful when it is used to conceal the natural relationship.

Adoption by natural single parents

98. There are a few cases† where a single woman adopts her own illegitimate child. A single woman has already, in law, the right to the custody of her child and a duty to maintain him. Adoption of the child does not confer upon her rights and responsibilities towards the child which she did not have before. The creation of an adoptive relationship cannot alter the facts that she was unmarried when the child was born, and that he was born illegitimate. In so far as the adoption is an attempt to hide the facts from the child it is likely in the long run to be damaging to him rather than helpful. It is important for a child to know the truth about his origins and some mothers may need help in telling him of his position.

99. Similar considerations apply to the adoption of an illegitimate child by his natural father alone, which is legally permissible but uncommon.‡ A putative father has not, in law, an automatic right to the custody of his child, and adoption gives him that right. However, the Legitimacy Act 1959 gave a putative father the right to apply for the custody of his child under the Guardianship of Infants Acts§ (now, in relation to England and Wales, the Guardianship of Minors Act 1971).

100. The adoption of an illegitimate child by one of his natural parents alone

---

* "Relatives", for most practical purposes, means natural parents and step-parents, grand-parents and uncles and aunts, although brothers and sisters and more distant relatives may adopt.
  † In 1970, 84 such orders were made in England and Wales and 5 in Scotland (see Appendix B, Table 2, for the ages of the children at adoption).
  ‡ In 1970, 11 such orders were made in England and Wales, and none in Scotland.
  § In Scotland he has this right under the Illegitimate Children (Scotland) Act 1930.

27

has one very important legal effect: it cuts out the other parent. In our working paper we put forward the view that it was undesirable that adoption should be used by a mother to cut the links between a child and his father, or by the father to cut the links between a child and his mother; that custody applications were the appropriate means of settling disputes between parents, whether married to each other or not; and that it followed that it should no longer be possible for a natural parent to adopt his or her own child.

101. Most witnesses, while agreeing that adoption by a natural parent alone was usually unnecessary and was to be discouraged, thought there were a few cases in which it might be in the interests of the welfare of the child. For example, if the natural mother had died, adoption by the putative father might give the child a greater feeling of security in his relationship with his father. There have also been cases were a natural mother has adopted her own child to protect herself from the anxiety caused by repeated and vexatious applications for guardianship made by a putative father. It was also argued that adoption by the mother makes the child a full member of her family for the purpose of inheritance on an intestacy, although extinguishing the child's right to inherit on the intestacy of the putative father. We think this is better dealt with by the making of wills, or by a change in the law of inheritance by illegitimate children, than by adoption.

102. We have come to the conclusion that there may be exceptional cases where adoption by a natural parent would be for the child's welfare. We think, however, that the law should require the applicant to satisfy the court that there are special circumstances which justify, as an exceptional measure, the making of an order. The court should be required to state the reasons for its opinion that there are special circumstances justifying an adoption order and to record those reasons. We think it follows that, where those special circumstances are present and an adoption order is made, any obligation of the father to pay maintenance should cease and any affiliation order (or, in Scotland, any decree of affiliation and aliment) be discharged, as in the case of adoption by persons other than the natural mother. We consider that the existing exception in section 15 of the 1958 Act in respect of adoption by a natural mother who is a single woman should be repealed.

Adoption by a parent and a step-parent

103. A large and increasing proportion of all adoption applications are made by a parent and a step-parent (see paragraph 97). The great majority of these applications are made by natural mothers married to step-fathers, a few by natural fathers married to step-mothers. (For convenience we refer in this section to natural mothers and step-fathers.) The numbers of illegitimate children and legitimate children adopted in this way are roughly equal.*

104. Where the mother of an illegitimate child has married a man who is not the child's father, and the couple apply jointly to adopt the child, the effect of the adoption is that the mother relinquishes her sole legal rights in relation

---

* In 1970, 5,202 legitimate children and 5,054 illegitimate children in England and Wales were adopted by a parent and step-parent. The corresponding figures for Scotland were 227 and 256 (see Appendix B, Table 2).

to the child, which become vested equally in her and her husband. Her own legal relationship to her child changes from the natural to the adoptive relationship. The motives behind such applications are generally simple—to change the child's name and birth certificate and to confer full legal rights and obligations on the step-father who wants to assume responsibility for the child.

105. Adoptions of legitimate children on the remarriage of a parent are increasing and the circumstances in these cases may be varied. We suggested in our working paper that it was desirable to recognise openly the fact and the consequences of divorce and of death; that one of these consequences is that many children are living with a parent and a step-parent; and that the legal extinguishment by adoption of a legitimate child's links with one half of his own family was inappropriate and could be damaging.

An alternative to adoption

106. At present adoption is the only way in which a step-parent may assume all the rights and obligations of a parent. We recommend, in Chapter 6, the extension of guardianship law to enable him to be appointed guardian of the child. The mother's legal relationship with the child would continue unchanged. If it were also desired to change the child's name, this could be done in England and Wales by simple deed or deed poll.* If the step-father wished the child to inherit from him, he could make a will. It thus seems that the aims referred to in paragraph 104, with the exception of a new birth certificate, could be achieved without the need for adoption at all, so avoiding the artificiality involved in adoption by a natural parent.

Should adoption by step-parents still be allowed?

107. Given the alternative of guardianship, should adoption by step-parents still be allowed? The step-father might feel that guardianship was not quite the same as being recognised in law as the child's parent. Adoption confers such recognition, and would achieve the aims in view by one step instead of by a number of separate steps. However, the disadvantages of severing a child from one half of his family (see paragraph 105) are such that we considered that there was less justification for permitting the adoption by a step-parent of a legitimate child of his spouse. We realised that this would make a distinction between legitimate and illegitimate children, and in our working paper we made a special request for further evidence on this issue.

108. The evidence we received was overwhelmingly opposed to our suggestion. Some witnesses pointed to the positive advantages of adoption to a legitimate child whose other parent is dead or where contact with that parent and his family is negligible or non-existent. Others were strongly opposed to the distinction between legitimate and illegitimate children, pointing out that a parent may have a legitimate and an illegitimate child and on the remarriage of the parent the illegitimate child could be adopted by the step-parent but not the legitimate child.

---

* In Scotland, the Registration of Births, Deaths and Marriages (Scotland) Act 1965 enables a person, including an adopted person, who has assumed a surname or other name which he has used regularly for a period of two years, to have this name recorded by the Registrar General. The birth certificates issued thereafter show both the new name and the name that it has replaced.

109. We have come to the conclusion that it would be wrong to distinguish between legitimate and illegitimate children, and that the law should not prohibit adoption by step-parents in either case. But we remain of the opinion that guardianship will be more appropriate in most cases. We recommend that whenever a step-parent applies to adopt a child of his spouse the court should first consider whether guardianship would be more appropriate in all the circumstances of the case, first consideration being given to the long-term welfare of the child.

110. Adoption by a step-father alone extinguishes his wife's rights and responsibilities. This is why applications have to be made jointly in these cases. Some mothers have objected to having to adopt their own children in order to confer rights and responsibilities on the step-father. In future a mother will not have to do so because the step-father will be able to apply for guardianship. A guardianship order will not extinguish the mother's legal rights and obligations but will result in her sharing them with her husband.

Adoption by relatives other than parents

111. The main objection to adoptions by other relatives is that legal relationships are created which differ from, and distort, the natural relationship not only of the adopters to the child but also of the child to his own parents. Where the real circumstances are hidden from the child, his discovery of them later may be even more damaging than in other adoptions; he may, for example, suddenly discover that his "parents" are really his grandparents, and his older "sister" is really his mother.

112. It is often in the interests of the child to be cared for by relatives and it is entirely natural for relatives to care for a child whose own parents cannot do so; they are already part of the family and do not need a court order to make them so. Legal recognition of the responsibility which relatives have undertaken towards the child, and legal security, can be obtained by guardianship. We therefore see guardianship, when it is extended to relatives as we recommend in Chapter 6, as the normal legal procedure for settling questions of custody as between parents and relatives, as well as between parents. In our working paper we said that there might be a few situations, especially when both the child's natural parents were dead, in which adoption by relatives might be thought more in the child's interests than guardianship, and we did not, therefore, suggest a complete prohibition of these adoptions.

113. In the main the evidence supported this view. Some witnesses would have prohibited all such adoptions, but others stressed the stability that adoption by relatives can give when the child is orphaned, and the greater protection it gives in other cases against subsequent reclaim by the natural parents. But where the mother and other relatives are likely to be in regular contact with the child, we doubt whether the nature of the order affects the reality of the situation, and the irrevocability of an adoption order may sometimes be a disadvantage. In most cases guardianship seems likely to provide the more realistic and acceptable solution, provision being made for access by the natural parents where this is desirable. Guardianship could protect a child from removal by a young unstable mother without distorting relationships, and would leave the way open for variation of the order if in later years this

was for the welfare of the child. Family circumstances may change, and a mother whose relationship with her child has not been distorted by adoption may later be able to offer him a stable home.

114. We consider that guardianship should normally be the appropriate means of recognising the position of relatives who seek to care for a child and of conferring legal security. We recommend that, as in the case of step-parents, the court hearing an adoption application by other relatives should first consider whether guardianship would be more appropriate in all the circumstances, first consideration being given to the long-term welfare of the child. For this purpose "relative" would be defined as in the 1958 Act.*

Recommendations

115. We accordingly *recommend* that:—

The law should require the court to be satisfied that there are special circumstances which justify as an exceptional measure the making of an order in favour of a natural parent alone, and these circumstances should be recorded by the court.

(Recommendation 18)

An adoption order granted to the natural mother alone should terminate any obligation of the putative father to make payments in respect of the child under an affiliation order, or decree of affiliation and aliment, or agreement, in the same way as does an adoption order granted to any other person.

(Recommendation 19)

In the light of recommendation 21 (that relatives caring for a child should be able to apply for guardianship), where a relative (including a step-parent applying jointly with his spouse) applies to adopt a child, the law should require the court first to consider whether guardianship would be more appropriate in all the circumstances of the case, first consideration being given to the long-term welfare of the child.

(Recommendation 20)

---

* "Relative" for the purposes of the Adoption Act 1958 means a grandparent, brother, sister, uncle or aunt, whether of full-blood or by affinity, and includes natural father.

CHAPTER 6

GUARDIANSHIP

116. There are many children who are not being brought up by their natural parents but are in the long-term care of foster parents or relatives. These people normally have no legal status in relation to the child, and the law provides no means by which they can obtain it without cutting his links with his natural family by adoption. They are faced with the choice of doing without the legal security, which may be damaging to the child, or applying for an adoption order. This is one reason why, as Chapter 5 has shown, adoption is frequently applied for in inappropriate circumstances, particularly by relatives.

117. The Guardianship of Minors Act 1971 (which, in respect of England and Wales, consolidated earlier guardianship legislation)* is, in general, restricted to

(a) the appointment and powers of guardians to act after the death of one or both of a child's parents—a person may be appointed a guardian for this purpose, by a parent, by will or by deed, and the courts need not be involved at all;

(b) the resolution of disputes between persons who already have a legal relationship with the child, e.g. between parents or between a surviving parent and a guardian appointed by will.

Most guardianship proceedings concern disputes between married couples about the custody or maintenance of their children. Guardianship law also enables the putative father of an illegitimate child to apply for custody, or access. A person who has no established parental or legal relationship with a child cannot apply to a court to be appointed the child's guardian (or, in Scotland, tutor) unless

(a) the child has no parent, no guardian and no person having parental rights with respect to him; or

(b) the court exercises its power to appoint, in certain circumstances, a guardian to act jointly with a surviving parent; it is only in these comparatively rare situations that relatives or foster parents caring for a child can apply for guardianship.

118. When an application is made to a court under the Guardianship of Minors Act 1971 (or the corresponding Scottish legislation) the court's powers are to make such order as to the custody of the child as the court thinks fit; to order the father to pay maintenance in respect of the child; and to order reasonable access to the child. (It is possible to grant custody to one person and care and control to someone else, for example, custody, involving decisions about matters such as schooling, might be granted to the father, although the child might live with and be brought up by the mother, or custody might

---

* The separate Guardianship of Infants Acts are still operative in Scotland.

be granted jointly to both parents with care and control to one.) All these orders may be varied or discharged by the court on a subsequent occasion. The power to award custody is in general terms and is not restricted to the parties to the dispute; and it appears that the court has power to award custody to a third party, even a non-relative, if it considers that course to be the best for the child's welfare,* although it has no power to order maintenance to be paid to the third party. We are pleased to note the Government's announcement of their intention to introduce legislation which will give the court power to call for a report from the local authority or probation officer before reaching a decision and, in exceptional circumstances, to make a supervision order or commit the child to the care of the local authority.

119. Section 1 of the Guardianship of Minors Act 1971† sets out the principles to be followed where the custody or upbringing of a minor (a child under 18 in England and Wales, under 16 in Scotland)‡ is in question. It provides that the court "shall regard the welfare of the minor as the first and paramount consideration and shall not take into consideration whether from any other point of view the claim of the father is superior to that of the mother, or the claim of the mother is superior to that of the father".

The extension of guardianship to relatives and foster parents

120. We suggested in our working paper that the right to apply for custody under guardianship legislation should be made available to relatives and foster parents already caring for a child, subject to certain limitations. The evidence we received strongly supported this, particularly in the case of relatives. International Social Service had reservations about guardianship because it might not be understood in some overseas countries, it would not confer on the child the nationality of the guardians, and it might not enable the child to accompany the guardians if they wished to emigrate. We see the relevance of these comments and this is one of the reasons why we have not proposed a complete ban on adoption by relatives (see Chapter 5). But many witnesses thought that guardianship would be more appropriate than adoption for most relatives, and we recommend that relatives should be able to apply for guardianship.

121. There were more reservations about guardianship for foster parents, but we think there are some circumstances where guardianship by foster parents would be appropriate. We have in mind situations where the parents are out of the picture, and the foster parents and the child wish to legalise and secure their relationship and be independent of the local authority or child care agency, but the child is old enough to have a sense of identity and wishes to keep this and retain his own name. There are also a few cases where the parents are actively in touch with the child and the foster parents, and where this bond is secure, but the parents recognise that they will never be able to provide a home for the child. There are other cases

---

* D'Alton v D'Alton (1878) 4PD 87.
† In Scotland, section 1 of the Guardianship of Infants Act 1925.
‡ See footnote on page 34.

in which for financial reasons the foster parents may feel unable to seek adoption but guardianship with financial assistance may be appropriate (see paragraphs 134 to 136 on financial aid).

122. There must be some restriction on the circumstances in which foster parents can apply for guardianship. While courts would not be likely to accede to an application by foster parents who had cared for a child for a short period, the natural parents ought not to be caused the anxiety of being involved in such proceedings. We therefore recommend that, as in the case of adoption (see paragraph 91), foster parents should not be allowed to apply for guardianship unless they have cared for the child for 12 months.

Effect of guardianship order

123. Although we see the orders granted as similar to existing custody orders, we think that the term "guardianship" would be more appropriate. A guardian would be in a similar position to a parent having custody of his child. He would be able to take all decisions regarding the child's upbringing, except that he would not be able to consent to adoption. Eligibility for family allowances and for tax relief would be as under the present law; that is, a guardian maintaining the child would receive an income tax child allowance in respect of the child, and family allowance, if eligible, unless the child's parents were paying sufficient towards the child's maintenance to retain the family allowance. A guardianship order would differ from an adoption order in that it would not be irrevocable, would not permanently extinguish parental rights, would not alter the child's relationship to the members of his natural family or extinguish his right to inherit from them. The natural parents would still be the parents in law, although their parental rights would be suspended. The court would have power to vary or revoke the order subsequently on the application of the natural parents or the guardian or, in certain circumstances, the local authority (see paragraph 133). It would be possible for the child's natural parents to keep in touch with him where this seemed appropriate and in the interests of his welfare, but their access to him would be under the control of the court. The child would retain his own name, unless he wished to be known by that of his guardians, in which case it could be changed informally, by simple assumption of the guardian's name, or in England and Wales, by deed poll; in Scotland, a change of name can be registered at Register House. He could inherit from his guardians only if they made a will in his favour. A guardianship order would be effective until the child reached the age of majority in England and Wales, or in Scotland until the child reached the age of 16.*

124. Where a guardianship order was made in respect of a child in the care of a local authority or voluntary society, the responsibility of the authority or society would have to come to an end since their quasi-parental

* In Scotland, at common law, children are "pupil children" until they attain the age of 12 in the case of a girl and 14 in the case of a boy. Thereafter they are minors (until they attain the age of majority at 18), and there is in Scotland a legal principle whereby minors are permitted to have control over their own persons. This principle has, however, been modified to some extent by statute law: of particular relevance in the present context is the Custody of Children (Scotland) Act 1939, which provides that the powers of any court to make orders as to the custody etc. of pupil children should extend to children up to the age of 16.

responsibility could not co-exist with that of the guardians. A guardianship order would have the effect of revoking an order committing a child to the care of a local authority; a child in care under section 1 of the Children Act 1948* would cease to be in care; and where a resolution assuming parental rights had been passed by the authority it would be revoked by the order. In the case of a child in the care of a voluntary society the Boarding Out Regulations would cease to apply, as would the obligation to return the child to the society if so requested.

Procedure

125. Since a guardianship order can be reviewed by the court at any time, we do not propose any formal provisions for the giving of parental consent. The parents of the child should be notified of the application, as well as the local authority and any other interested person or body (including a local authority or voluntary society having care of the child), and they should all be parties to the application, with a right to attend and be heard. The court would then establish, by questioning the parents if they were present, or by appropriate evidence if they were not, whether they agreed to the granting of the application; this would be one of the matters to be covered in the social enquiry report. In cases where one or both natural parents were not present and could not be notified of the hearing, the court should be able to proceed with the application on being satisfied that the parents could not be found, or, in the case of the putative father of an illegitimate child, that his identity was not known, or that he was not maintaining, and had had no recent contact with, the child. The making of a guardianship order should not be dependent on the agreement of one or both parents, although the court would have to take their wishes into account.

126. We envisage that most guardianship orders would be made with the agreement of the natural parent, and that a natural parent who was unwilling to consent to the final severance of legal ties by an adoption order would sometimes be willing to consent to guardianship. But where a foster parent has cared for a child for 5 years, we consider that the position should be the same in respect of guardianship applications as with applications to adopt (see paragraph 164) and that the position should be frozen, so that, once an application had been made to the court, the child could not be removed without the leave of the court.

127. In deciding whether to make a guardianship order the court would be required to follow the principle in the existing guardianship law and regard the welfare of the child as the first and paramount consideration. In deciding whether an order would be for the child's welfare, the court would be able to consider all the relevant factors, including the wishes of the child, where he was old enough to form a view; the wishes of his parents; and the suitability of the applicants.

128. To assist the court in deciding what order to make, we consider that it should be provided with a social enquiry report about the circumstances of the child and the applicants. We recommend that applicants for a guardianship

---

* In Scotland section 15 of the Social Work (Scotland) Act 1968.

order should be required to give the local authority notice of their intention to apply, and an order should not be made until at least three months have elapsed from the date of notification. It would be the duty of the local authority to investigate the family situation, including the matters referred to in the foregoing paragraph, and furnish the court with a report.

129. The Guardianship of Minors Act 1971,* if amended as the Government propose, will give courts the power to make a supervision order in conjunction with a guardianship order. This will rarely be appropriate in the case of a child boarded out by a local authority or voluntary society because, if the authority or society consider that the applicants need continuing support and guidance, and they satisfy the court that this is so, the appropriate course will often be to refuse the application rather than grant it in conjunction with a supervision order. There will also be power to commit a child to the care of the local authority in exceptional circumstances.

130. We consider that, as in other custody applications under the Guardianship of Minors Act, it should be open to the court to make an order for maintenance payments by the natural parents or parent. In some cases where the parents are out of the picture and do not wish to have access to the child it would clearly be inappropriate to expect them to contribute. In cases where the parents wish to have regular access to the child and have a real interest in him, some contribution by them, however small, might be ordered; the guardians would be more likely to co-operate willingly in arranging for the parents to have access to the child if they knew they were contributing to the child's maintenance. In some cases parents may be overseas and wish to arrange for a guardian to have full powers while the parents themselves continue to meet the full costs of the child's maintenance. We envisage that circumstances will vary widely, but that the courts can be relied upon to exercise their discretion in deciding what order, if any, to make in respect of the child's maintenance.

Revocation of guardianship orders

131. An essential feature of guardianship, by contrast to adoption, is that it does not finally cut the child's links with his natural parents; it is subject to review by the court; and it may be revoked if this is in the child's welfare.

132. If an order is made against the wishes of the parents, and they find difficulty in accepting the decision, the guardians may require some protection against frequent applications for revocation of the order when there has been no material change in the circumstances. We therefore recommend that the court should have discretion not to proceed with an application where the court is satisfied that there has been no significant change in circumstances since a recent application; that no injustice would be done; and that the child and guardians need protection against the uncertainty and distress they might otherwise be caused.

133. There will inevitably be some cases in which guardianship will break down. While most adoption orders are made in respect of babies, many of

---

* In Scotland, the Guardianship of Infants Acts.

the children for whom guardianship is sought will be older children who have had a number of different homes and disturbing experiences and, while they may appear to have settled well at the time the guardianship order is made, difficulties may arise later. It might be necessary for the child to be received into the care of the local authority. In that case we recommend that the local authority should be able to apply to a court for the order to be revoked, or varied.

Financial aid

134. Many of the persons who wish to become guardians will be in receipt of a boarding out allowance from a local authority or a voluntary society, and would not be able to care for the child without some financial help. In our working paper we made a special request for comments on the possibility of allowances and subsidies for guardians and adoptive parents. We deal with adopters in Chapter 4. There was considerable support for allowances for guardians.

135. The Association of Municipal Corporations thought that guardians, like adopters, should rely for financial assistance on tax relief and family allowances. One local authority, on the other hand, thought it reasonable that allowances should be paid since guardianship with financial support would prevent a number of children from coming into local authority care. The County Councils Association thought it arguable that allowances should be payable, at a standard minimum with the possibility of additional payments as necessary, to guardians whose means were inadequate. Some witnesses who were in favour of allowances for guardians would have preferred payment from central government funds. Others considered that caution would be necessary to avoid applicants whose motive was pecuniary; they saw as suitable recipients couples with several children who would like to care for one more but whose family budget was already stretched.

136. We do not see much danger of applications for guardianship in the hope of financial gain. In the case of children in care, local authorities and voluntary societies would be unlikely to pay more than the boarding out allowance and possibly less. Some children in the care of grandparents of limited means are received into care by the local authority and boarded out with the grandparents so that a boarding out allowance can be paid. We think that where conditions are otherwise satisfactory it should not be necessary to receive the child into care, and supervise the home, solely in order to pay an allowance. We therefore recommend that local authorities should be empowered to pay allowances to guardians. The court would have to be told in advance whether a local authority or voluntary society was prepared to pay an allowance to the applicants if an order were granted. The local authority making the social enquiry report would have to cover the financial situation in the report and indicate whether there was a need for financial assistance and whether they or a voluntary society were prepared to meet it. The amount might be reviewed annually by the authority or society in the light of any change in the family circumstances. The allowance would be to alleviate any financial hardship and not paid as of right like a boarding out allowance.

Applications for adoption where guardianship may be more appropriate

137. It is possible that, initially at any rate, there will be many applications for adoption orders by relatives, and some by foster parents, in circumstances where the court is likely to consider guardianship more appropriate. We think that it should be one of the duties of the local authority to point out to the applicants that guardianship is a possible alternative, to discuss this with them and to establish whether there are any special circumstances which make adoption more appropriate. If there appear to be no such special circumstances the applicants may decide to vary their application and seek guardianship instead of adoption. Others may wish the application to stand, but at the hearing the court may decide that adoption is not appropriate, although it would be prepared to consider favourably an application for guardianship. In these circumstances, the court would be able to explain the position to the applicants and give them an opportunity to consider whether they wished to apply for guardianship.

Recommendations

138. The law should provide a means, short of adoption, whereby relatives (and in some circumstances foster parents) already caring for a child may obtain legal recognition of their relationship with the child. Accordingly *we recommend* that:—

The right to apply for custody under the Guardianship of Minors Act 1971* (which we call, for convenience, "guardianship") should be extended for this purpose to relatives already caring for a child and foster parents, but it should not be open to foster parents to apply until they have cared for the child for at least twelve months.

(Recommendation 21)

A guardianship order should not deprive the natural parents of the right to consent, or withhold consent, to adoption. Subject to this, it should give the guardian parental powers and obligations, but the court should have the power to make an order for access by the parents, and to make a maintenance order where appropriate.

(Recommendation 22)

When guardians are appointed by a court for a child in the care of a local authority or voluntary organisation, he should thereby cease to be in their care, and any court order committing him to care or resolution assuming parental rights should lapse on the making of the guardianship order.

(Recommendation 23)

Applicants should be required to notify the local authority of their intention to apply for guardianship, and an order should not be made until at least three months have elapsed from the date of notification. The local authority should investigate the circumstances and furnish a report to the court.

(Recommendation 24)

The child's parents, the local authority, and any other interested person

---

* In Scotland, the Guardianship of Infants Acts.

or body, should be a party to such a guardianship application, with a right to be heard before the court takes its decision.

(Recommendation 25)

The powers of the courts in dealing with guardianship applications should include, in exceptional circumstances, power to make a supervision order whether or not it grants the application, and to commit the child to the care of the local authority on refusing the application.

(Recommendation 26)

Parents should have the right to apply at any time for the revocation of a guardianship order so that the child may return to them, but the court should have discretion not to proceed with such applications if they are made repeatedly where there has been no change in circumstances.

(Recommendation 27)

A local authority should have power to apply for a revocation or variation of a guardianship order in respect of a child received into its care.

(Recommendation 28)

Local authorities should have power to pay allowances to persons who are granted guardianship orders if there is a need for financial assistance.

(Recommendation 29)

CHAPTER 7

FOSTER CHILDREN

139. At the time of our appointment concern had been expressed about a number of children who had been reclaimed by their natural parents after many years in foster homes, and we were asked to consider the position of long-term foster parents* who wished to keep a child permanently, by adoption or otherwise, against the wish of the natural parent.

140. The circumstances in which children are fostered vary widely. Many are boarded out by local authorities or voluntary organisations. Others are placed privately by their parents. A large number are placed for periods as short as a few weeks to meet a temporary family crisis, such as the confinement or illness of the mother. In other cases it seems likely, at the time of placement, that the child will have to be boarded out for a considerable period. Very often the future cannot be clearly seen and what was thought likely to be a short term placement may last much longer, or vice versa.

141. The conflict situations which we were asked to consider, and which give rise to so much publicity, arise in only a very small minority of cases (see Appendix D), but we are deeply concerned about them because they can cause much distress to parents, foster parents and, above all, the children. Yet because foster care is used for children in such a wide variety of circumstances there is a risk that measures taken to protect a small number of children might create problems for others. The issues are complex and no change in the law will itself provide a complete solution.

The present law

142. There is nothing in the present adoption law which treats foster parents differently from other applicants. They have the same right to apply for adoption as others, although it appeared from the evidence we received that not everybody knew of this. This means that, like other applicants, they have to obtain the consent of the natural parent or parents, or ask the court to dispense with it on one of the statutory grounds.

143. When a mother asks to have her baby placed for adoption she signs a consent form at an early stage and this is presented to the court with the adoption application. The law provides that once this form has been presented to the court, the mother may not remove the child from the care of the applicants without the leave of the court. The situation is thus frozen until the court hearing. But where the parents have never considered adoption, and consequently have never signed a consent form, as will be the case

---

* By foster parents we mean persons who are caring for a child boarded out with them by a local authority or voluntary society, not for the purpose of adoption, or placed with them privately by the child's parents who will usually, but not invariably, be paying for the child's maintenance.

where a child has been placed for fostering, the situation is not frozen. It is open to the foster parents to ask the court to dispense with the parent's consent on one of the statutory grounds (see paragraph 205), but this might result in the mother reclaiming the child, which she is free to do, and the application could not then proceed. For this reason local authorities, voluntary societies and foster parents may hesitate to broach the subject of adoption, unless they are confident that the parents will agree. The result is that, unless the child has been boarded out with the foster parents by a local authority which has parental rights, he may be reclaimed without notice at any time.

The suggestions in our working paper

144. We suggested in our working paper that where foster parents had cared for a child for five years they should be able to apply to the court for adoption and the position should be frozen pending the court hearing even if the mother had not consented. In cases where the child had been in their care for between one and five years we suggested that foster parents should be able to apply with the consent of the local authority, and that the position should be frozen pending the authority's decision and, if it consented, pending the application to the court.

The reaction to our suggestions

145. These suggestions attracted far more comment than any others. While they received considerable support from members of the public, many professional organisations in the child care field, such as the British Association of Social Workers and the Society of Medical Officers of Health, and some large voluntary child care organisations, such as Dr Barnardo's and the Church of England Children's Society, disagreed with them. Different witnesses gave different reasons, but arguments which frequently recurred may be summarised as follows.

(a) It was argued that fostering is only one method of accommodating children in care and that, under our provisional suggestions, the position of the natural parents would have varied according to the accommodation arranged for the child. If the child were boarded out, the possibility that the link would be cut by adoption, against the wishes of the natural parent, would be greater than where the child was accommodated in a children's home. This might cause parents some anxiety about leaving their children in care if the local authority boarded them out. Some witnesses said that if it did not spell the end of fostering it could well lead to some reduction in it, which would deprive some children of the form of care which would best meet their needs.

(b) Many witnesses stressed that fostering and adoption were different. Fostering offered a service to children while retaining, if possible, their links with their natural parents. Adoption, on the other hand, meant the complete severance of the ties with the natural parents. It was argued that some people might have the qualities for fostering, particularly with good social work support, while not meeting the different criteria for adoptive parents. Moreover, where a child was privately placed, the foster home was not professionally selected and was subject only to the limited powers of local authorities, under section 6 of the Children Act 1958, to prohibit persons from acting as foster parents.

41

(c) A number of witnesses said that foster parents might come to think that they would acquire a "right" to adopt with the passage of time, and that this might lead them to try to weaken the links with the natural parents instead of maintaining them.

(d) We were told that our suggested time limits were arbitrary, and that natural parents could evade them by reclaiming their children shortly before the time expired.

(e) It was said that our suggestions stemmed from consideration of a few well publicised cases which might have been prevented by better casework or use of the power to assume parental rights. Where there had been little parental contact it was not necessarily the fault of the natural parents, since foster parents may have actively discouraged such contacts, and local authorities or voluntary societies may not have done enough to encourage them. The remedy suggested was better casework with foster children, foster parents and natural parents, enlargement of the power to assume parental rights, and more frequent use of this power.

(f) Some thought that the requirement for local authority consent within five years would provoke conflict situations between local authorities and foster parents. Our provisional suggestion that the appropriate way for foster parents to challenge the local authority's decision was through elected representatives was said to be unrealistic.

146. To sum up, there was a strong body of opinion, particularly from those experienced in the child care field, that the effect of our proposals would be to increase the number of "tugs-of-war" between natural parents and foster parents in the courts; that the result would be a reduction in the number of children fostered and an increase in the number accommodated in children's homes, or kept by their mothers even if their situation was such that it was in the children's interest to be fostered; and thus changes in the law designed to further the welfare of some children might be harmful to the welfare of many others. It was argued that the number of cases in which children were reclaimed against their interests (see paragraph 153) did not justify putting at risk the whole fostering system.

147. We were aware of these risks and it was for this reason that we thought that, unless the foster parents had cared for the child for five years, a sifting process was desirable before cases could come to court. To achieve this we suggested that local authority consent should be necessary. But if, as most witnesses thought, it would be necessary to give a right of appeal to the court against the local authority decision, the sifting process which we suggested would be less effective. Moreover, we accept that there is force in the argument that, where the foster parents were not allowed to proceed, their relationship with the boarding out authority would be impaired. We have decided, therefore, not to pursue this suggestion.

An alternative approach

148. In the light of the evidence we received, and of our discussions with witnesses about it (which took up a large part of the time we spent taking oral evidence) and of our own lengthy consideration of this complex problem, we now put forward recommendations based on an alternative approach. We

start from the position that a child may be reclaimed by a parent who is a stranger, at short notice (or with no notice at all) without any opportunity for consideration of the position. This applies to all children in care and not just to those boarded out with foster parents. The sudden removal of a child from a children's home where he has established good relationships may be equally damaging. Some of the recommendations we make therefore apply to all children in care. Some of our recommendations still include time limits and we see no way of avoiding them when the length of time in care has become an important factor in the child's situation.

Fostering practice

149. We are satisfied that, in some of the cases which give rise to concern, better practice and more use of existing powers might have prevented the situation from developing into a legal tussle over the child. Social conditions, such as a shortage of housing, have led to children being received into care at short notice, and the shortage of social workers, and a lack of vacancies in residential children's homes, have led to instances of foster parents being hastily recruited for an urgent and supposedly temporary need which has developed into long-term foster care of the child placed in their home. In our view foster parents need to be very carefully selected for the skilled job of caring for a child in trust for the parents. They should be encouraged to work together with the social worker and to further, in the majority of cases, the aim of rehabilitating the child in his natural family.

150. The fostering practice of local authorities and voluntary societies was outside our terms of reference, and we did not consider it appropriate to institute a wide ranging enquiry on a matter which is only marginal to adoption law and procedure. We think that in the long-term, improvements in practice will, in the main, depend upon significant increases in the number of qualified social workers available to local authorities. In the short-term, however, we hope that the central departments will consider as a matter of urgency what else can be done to secure improvements in fostering practice, whether by the issue of written guidance, as was done for adoption in "A Guide to Adoption Practice", or by other means. We also make two specific recommendations for improved practice.

An explanatory leaflet

151. Good practice requires that, when a child is received into care, his needs should be explained to the parents, including the likelihood of his forming attachments with substitute parents which it might not be desirable to break, and which might have to be legally recognised if the parents fail to keep in touch with him. As an aid to good practice we recommend that an explanatory leaflet should be given, and explained orally wherever practicable, to the parents of every child coming into care, in the same way as a memorandum is given and explained to the parents of every child placed for adoption. The central departments might prepare a model explanatory leaflet covering the needs of the child and the rights and obligations of all concerned. We think that better communication of this sort, coupled with improvements in practice generally, would do much to prevent some of the more difficult tug-of-war situations arising.

Notice of removal

152. At present the parents of a child received into local authority care may require his return at any time, irrespective of the length of time he has been in care, provided that parental rights have not been assumed. A sudden move, without preparation, can be damaging to the child and may have long-term repercussions. We therefore recommend that where the child has been in care for more than one year there should be a requirement to give 28 days notice of removal. Removal within the period of notice, without permission, would be prohibited in the same way as removal of a child subject to a care order. 28 days would be a maximum period of notice, which could be waived by the authority or voluntary society, who, in many cases, would be likely to agree to the child being returned in a much shorter period. This provision would help to prevent impulsive and temporary removals from care, and would give time for the child and parents to get to know each other again.

Assumption of parental rights

153. Many witnesses suggested that the interests of children could be protected by a greater readiness on the part of local authorities to assume parental rights. Information obtained by the Home Office from local authorities in England and Wales about children reclaimed by parents in 1968, against the local authority's strong advice, showed that reclaims were few where full use was made of the power to assume parental rights; that more use could have been made of these provisions; but that in some situations the existing powers were inadequate (see Appendix D for further information about this survey). A later survey of children reclaimed in 1970 (see paragraph 162) gave some reason to think that casework had improved, and encouraged us to believe that the power to assume parental rights could be used constructively to phase a return to parents where this seemed desirable; more effort was being put into retaining contacts between children and their parents, so that there was less likelihood of a child being reclaimed by a parent who was a stranger to him. Nevertheless there may be cases where it is not in the child's interest to be returned, or to be returned at that point of time, and it seems to us that the existing grounds for assumption of parental rights are not always adequate.

154. Section 2 of the Children Act 1948 enables a local authority to assume parental rights over a child in their care where it appears to them:

(a) that his parents are dead and that he has no guardian; or

(b) that a parent or guardian . . . has abandoned* him or suffers from some permanent disability rendering the said person incapable of caring for the child, or is of such habits or mode of life as to be unfit to have the care of the child.

These grounds were extended by section 48 of the Children and Young Persons Act 1963 to include the following grounds:

(a) that the parent or guardian suffers from a mental disorder (within the meaning of the Mental Health Act 1959 or the Mental Health (Scotland) Act 1960) which renders him unfit to have the care of the child; or

---

* Section 48(1) of the Children and Young Persons Act 1963 provides that, where a child is in care and the whereabouts of his parents or guardian have remained unknown for not less than 12 months, he shall be deemed abandoned for the purposes of assuming parental rights.

(b) that the parent or guardian has so persistently failed without reasonable cause to discharge the obligations of a parent or guardian as to be unfit to have the care of the child.*

155. Parental rights are assumed by a resolution passed by the local authority. If a parent has not consented to the resolution it is open to him to object, in writing, and if he does so the resolution lapses unless confirmed by a court.† The assumption of parental rights does not give the local authority the right to consent to adoption.

156. We think it would be an advantage, if in addition to these grounds, local authorities had a discretionary power to assume parental rights in respect of any child who had been in their care for a continuous period of three years. This would provide machinery for local authority intervention at a time when the parents, for whatever reason, have not been undertaking parental care for a considerable period, and at a stage in the history of a child in care where decisions as to his long-term future may be required. We think that to give local authorities this power after a shorter period, without the need to establish any other ground, would constitute an unwarranted threat to parents of children in care, while a period of more than three years would be too long in the life of a child. As at present, a parent would be able to challenge the local authority decision before the court, which should be required to consider not only whether the necessary three years period had elapsed, but also whether the continuation of the resolution would be for the long-term welfare of the child. It would need to be made clear that occasional visits to parents of short duration should not be treated as breaking a continuous period. Local authorities should still assume parental rights at an earlier stage where any of the existing grounds apply.

157. We consider that there should be power to retain in care a child in respect of whom parental rights can be assumed in regard to one parent only. We have in mind the situation where a mentally ill mother may not, on discharge from hospital, be sufficiently recovered to have the care of her child; she may even need further periods in hospital. Yet the father against whom parental rights cannot be taken may exercise his right to withdraw his child from care, thus returning him to the care of his wife despite her continuing incapacity. We recommend that where parental rights have been assumed in respect of one parent, the local authority should be empowered to retain a child in care so as to prevent his return to the care of a parent in respect of whom parental rights have been assumed.

158. There was general agreement with the suggestion in our working paper that means should be found to safeguard children in the care of voluntary child care agencies in cases where it was desirable to assume parental rights. There was less agreement on how this should be done. Some voluntary societies considered that they were just as accountable to the public as local authorities, and should therefore be free to assume parental rights in the same way. They recognised that a resolution by a voluntary society would not have the same standing as one passed by a local authority, but suggested that in the

---

* There are similar provisions in Scottish law (section 16 of the Social Work (Scotland) Act 1968).
† Section 2(2) and (3) of the Children Act 1948.

case of voluntary societies application should be made to a court for parental rights to be conferred. However, the object of the procedure in the case of children in the care of local authorities is to avoid court proceedings. If, for example, the mother has had a mental breakdown, assumption of parental rights by resolution may be less distressing than application to a court. We recommend that, where a child is in the care of a voluntary society, the local authority in whose area the child is resident should be empowered, at the request of the voluntary society, to pass a resolution assuming parental rights, the grounds being similar to those applying to children in the care of local authorities. We do not think it would be appropriate to expect the local authority to take over financial responsibility in every case, and we envisage that the local authority could assume parental rights on the understanding that the voluntary society continued to care for the child.

159. Where a parent objects to a resolution assuming parental rights, and the court upholds the resolution, the parents have no right of appeal to a higher court. We recommend that there should be a right of appeal in such circumstances.

Applications to free a child for adoption

160. In Chapter 8 we consider at some length the needs of children in the care of local authorities or registered adoption agencies whose parents cannot bring themselves to make a long-term plan for them (paragraphs 220 to 223). We recommend in that chapter that it should be open to the authority or agency to apply to the court for the permanent transfer of parental rights so that the child is free for adoption. This procedure would be available for children boarded out with foster parents, as well as for children in residential establishments, but the initiative would rest with the local authority or adoption agency and not with foster parents. It would be necessary to satisfy the court that the parents' consent should be dispensed with on one of the statutory grounds.

Application to adopt by foster parents who have cared for a child for five years

161. We think that the arguments summarised in paragraph 143 have much less force in relation to foster parents who have cared for a child for five years. The remoter possibility of an adoption application by foster parents in five years' time is less likely to deter natural parents from allowing their children to be fostered. It does not follow that an adoption order will be appropriate in every case, or even in most cases, where foster parents have cared for a child for five years, but there is a strong *prima facie* case for enabling an application for adoption to be made and considered by the courts without the risk of the child being suddenly removed.

162. The number of children who have been boarded out in the same foster home for more than five years is considerable. We obtained information from 18 local authorities in England and Wales, four in Scotland and three voluntary societies in order to form an estimate of the number of children who might be affected. The authorities were selected on a random sampling basis with the help of the Home Office Research Unit. On 31 December 1970

there were 2,354 children boarded out by these 25 authorities and societies who had been in the same foster home for more than five years. During the year 1970, 38 children who had been in care for more than five years had been discharged from their care, and in only two cases did the agency concerned consider that it would have been in the interests of the child to remain in the foster home (see Appendix D).

163. We have considered whether our recommendation on this point should apply to foster children placed privately by their parents. The parents of a privately fostered child remain fully responsible for him, in the majority of cases making regular payments for his upkeep, and there is usually no doubt about their intention to resume caring for him as soon as they are able. The circumstances in which these children are placed vary widely; they include, for example, children whose parents arrange for them to be cared for while working overseas. In other cases the child is placed with foster parents while the parents (often from overseas) are following a course of study in this country, and the Home Office, in the 1967 report on the work of the Children's Department, referred to the increase in these cases and said that the "heavy demand makes it difficult for some parents to be discriminating". Moreover, there is only limited control over these placements.* Nevertheless, if a child has been with private foster parents for a period as long as five years, we think that they should be in the same position as other foster parents.

164. We adhere to our provisional proposition that foster parents who have cared for a child for five years or more should be entitled to apply to the court for adoption, in the knowledge that the position would be frozen until the application was heard, irrespective of the views of the natural parents or of any local authority or voluntary society in whose care the child may be. It would still be for the court to consider whether there were grounds for dispensing with the parent's consent, and whether an adoption order would be in the interests of the welfare of the child, bearing in mind the child's own wishes if he were old enough to form a view. Any local authority or voluntary society having care of the child would be a respondent to the application, with a right to be heard. We suggest that the position should be frozen from the time the foster parents notify their intention to apply to adopt, and the "freezing" should lapse after three months if a formal application for an adoption order had not then been lodged. We recommend that a similar provision should apply to applications for guardianship by foster parents who have cared for a child for five years or more (see paragraph 126).

Conclusion

165. Although legal tussles between parents and foster parents occur in only a small minority of cases, they cause much distress, particularly to the child, and have given rise to legitimate public concern. The situations in which they arise are extremely complex and are, in our view, incapable of any single broad and simple solution. As our study of this problem progressed, we became increasingly aware of the need to avoid recommending changes which might create difficulties in the thousands of unpublicised cases in which children are

---

* The local authority has no control over selection, apart from power to prohibit totally unsuitable persons from acting as foster parents.

successfully fostered. With this in mind, we have put forward a combination of recommendations which, if implemented together, will safeguard the welfare of foster children and afford greater security to foster parents generally, without weakening the confidence of parents in the fostering system.

Recommendations

166. *We recommend* that:—

An explanatory leaflet should be given to the parents of every child received into care.

(Recommendation 30)

The law should require 28 days' notice of removal of a child who has been in the care of a local authority for 12 months or more, and during this period of notice it should not be possible to remove the child without the permission of the caring authority.

(Recommendation 31)

Local authorities should have discretion to resolve to assume parental rights over any child who has been in their care for three years. If such a decision were challenged, the court should be required to consider not only whether the three years period had elapsed, but also whether the continuation of the resolution would be for the child's welfare.

(Recommendation 32)

The grounds for assumption of parental rights should be extended to protect children where rights may be assumed in respect of one parent and not the other.

(Recommendation 33)

Local authorities should have power to assume parental rights in respect of children in the care of a voluntary society, if the society so requests.

(Recommendation 34)

There should be a right of appeal from the decision of a juvenile court to uphold a resolution assuming parental rights.

(Recommendation 35)

Local authorities and registered adoption societies should be able to apply to a court for the permanent transfer of parental rights so that the child is free for adoption (see paragraphs 220 to 223 and Recommendation 53).

Where foster parents who have cared for a child for five years or more apply for an adoption or guardianship order, the natural parents should not be able to remove the child before the hearing without the leave of the court.

(Recommendation 36)

CHAPTER 8

CONSENT TO ADOPTION
(including dispensing with consent and the rights of the putative father)

167. The present law prohibits the making of an adoption order without the consent of every person who is a parent* or guardian of the child (section 4 of the Adoption Act 1958), unless the court dispenses with consent on one of the seven grounds specified in section 5 of the Act. Evidence of consent may be given by personal attendance at the court hearing the adoption application, or by the signing of a consent document suitably attested. The consent of a mother is not valid if given before the child is six weeks old. Consent may be given without knowing the identity of the proposed adopters, and may be given unconditionally, or subject to conditions with respect to the religious persuasion in which the infant is proposed to be brought up. If the consent document has been signed and an application for an adoption order is pending in any court, the parent or guardian who signed the document may not remove the child from the applicant without the consent of the court (section 34 of the Adoption Act 1958).† It is the duty of the guardian ad litem to ascertain that every consent to adoption has been freely given‡ and with full understanding of the nature of an adoption order. It is open to the parent or guardian to withdraw consent at any time before an adoption order is made, subject to the court's discretion to dispense with consent (see paragraph 205). A minimum of three months' care and possession of the child is necessary before an order can be made, so that consent may be withdrawn when the applicants have already cared for the child for several months, or even longer.

168. There appear to be no grounds for departure from the two basic principles in the existing law: that adoption should normally be possible only with parental consent; and that it should be open to a court to dispense with consent on certain specified grounds. But there is considerable dissatisfaction with the timing and nature of the present consent procedure. Parental rights and obligations are not terminated at the time the parent signs the consent document. They continue until an adoption order is made some weeks or months later. The argument in favour of this system is that there is never a period when the child is not the legal responsibility of either natural or adoptive parents. But there is evidence that this procedure imposes unnecessary strain and confusion on the mother. Moreover, it may encourage indecisiveness on her part; and by maintaining her legal responsibility for the child until the adoption order is made, it may prevent her from facing the

---

* The mother of the child may herself be a minor, but, however young, she is fully competent to consent to her child's adoption and the consent of her parents is not required. A putative father of an illegitimate child is not a parent for the purpose of giving consent to adoption (see *Re M* (an infant) [1955] 2 QB 479).

† The Survey of Adoption in Great Britain[1] showed that in 98 per cent of applications by non-relatives the mother's consent was attached to the application; in the remaining 2 per cent of cases there was a request to dispense with her consent.

‡ This is not specifically required of the curator ad litem under the Scottish rules.

reality of her decision and planning her own future. This period of uncertainty can be considerably prolonged if there is a delay in the adoption arrangements.

169. The disadvantages for the adoptive parents are obvious. The welfare of the child is at risk while his future remains in doubt and there is a possibility that he may be moved. Even though this happens only in a small minority of cases, the knowledge that it is possible may give rise to anxiety on the part of all prospective adopters, who may hesitate to give total commitment to a child whom they may not be allowed to keep.

170. We suggested in our working paper that in agency cases it should be possible for consent to become final before an adoption order was made. We outlined a system similar to that followed in some overseas countries, notably many states in the United States of America, which enables parents to take an irrevocable decision to give up their child for adoption, and to relinquish parental rights and obligations, before the child is placed. These rights and obligations are transferred by the court to an adoption agency, and in due course are transferred by the agency to the adopters when an adoption order is made. This enables the mother to give up parental rights and obligations before an adoption order is made, while providing for their exercise by the agency in the meantime.

171. Our proposals found general acceptance, subject to reservations on three points:
(a) Many witnesses doubted whether mothers would be willing to attend a court hearing for the purpose of relinquishing parental rights.
(b) It was thought that not all mothers who wished to have their child adopted through an agency would wish to give a general consent to adoption through a relinquishment procedure as distinct from consenting to adoption by a specific couple.
(c) The majority of witnesses thought that, if it proved impossible to arrange for the adoption of a child in respect of whom parental rights had been transferred to an agency, the mother should be able to resume care of the child if she wished to do so.
These arguments have influenced the recommendations we now put forward.

172. We have tried to devise a system which will provide flexibility and choice, protection for the mother against hasty, ill-considered decisions or pressure from other people, and protection for the child and adoptive parents from undue delay and uncertainty. Our recommendations have also been influenced by the findings of the research carried out by Miss Raynor and Dr Triseliotis into the attitudes and wishes of the mothers themselves.[5, 6]

Relinquishment
173. We propose that it should be possible for the mother* and the adoption agency jointly to apply to the court for an order transferring parental rights and obligations to an agency with a view to the child's adoption. The court's role when hearing the application would be a safeguarding one. It would have to satisfy itself.

---

* See note on page 2.

(a) that the mother, after considering the alternatives and implications, had freely made her decision to relinquish parental rights and obligations with a view to the child's adoption;

(b) that the child fulfilled the legal criteria for adoption (e.g. that he was resident in this country) and that the rights and interests of other persons (e.g. a putative father or a mother's husband) had been considered.

So long as the court was satisfied about these matters, it would be required to grant the application. It would be open to the court, if it was not satisfied, to adjourn the case for further enquiries.

174. We accept the view of many witnesses that attendance at a formal court hearing might be viewed by parents (particularly unmarried mothers) with much anxiety. The transfer of parental rights would have to be effected by a court, but we propose that the court should have discretion to proceed in the absence of the mother and the agency.

175. Where the mother's presence was not required we do not think that the court should proceed on the basis of the application alone. We consider that it should have separate written evidence of her decision to relinquish parental rights. There is considerable dissatisfaction with the existing procedure, under which a parent's written consent to adoption is witnessed by a single justice or court officer. Miss Raynor's research showed that the form was often signed in surroundings and in a manner inappropriate to so serious a step, for example, over the counter of a busy court office.[5] In any event, besides evidence of the mother's decision to relinquish parental rights, it would be necessary to provide the court with evidence about the other matters referred to in paragraph 173, and we suggest the following procedure.

176. The mother and the agency would jointly apply to the court for relinquishment and for an order transferring parental rights to the agency; the agency would forward with the application a report explaining the steps which had been taken to help the mother to reach her decision. The court would then fix the date and time for consideration of the application and appoint an officer to interview the mother and the agency separately and, if necessary, together. The officer's duty would be to ascertain whether the mother, after considering the alternatives and implications, had freely made a decision to relinquish parental rights. For convenience we call this officer the "reporting officer", and we suggest that he should be drawn from the panel of senior social workers from whom we recommend that guardians ad litem should be drawn (see paragraph 254). The court would appoint a member of the panel unconnected with the agency making joint application with the mother.

177. The mother who wished to relinquish her parental rights, and transfer them to an adoption agency with a view to her child's adoption, would sign a form to this effect, the terms of which would be prescribed by rules of court. The reporting officer would witness the mother's signature and forward the form to the court with a report stating whether he was satisfied that the mother, after considering the alternatives and implications, had freely reached this decision. It would be a matter of good practice for the reporting officer to keep in touch with the agency, but rules of court should require him to inform the agency whether or not the mother had signed the form.

178. The reporting officer would inform the mother of the date and time fixed by the court for considering the application and explain that it was open to her to attend the court or not. If she intimated that she did not wish to attend, she would be able to sign a statement to this effect, which the reporting officer would also forward to the court. This would not prevent her subsequently deciding to attend the court, but we think that it would be helpful to the court to know whether the mother was likely to attend the hearing.

179. The mother would not be able to sign the form signifying her agreement to relinquish parental rights until the child was six weeks old (see paragraph 190). This would not prevent an application for relinquishment being made earlier, but the court would have to fix a date for the hearing which would give time for the reporting officer to obtain the mother's signature once the child was six weeks old and forward the documents to the court. If the reporting officer found that it would not be possible to complete the arrangements in time, he would ask the court to fix a later date. This might arise, for example, where it was necessary to give a putative father notice of the hearing. We consider the position of the putative father in paragraphs 192 to 198.

180. It would be for the court to decide, after consideration of the reports from the agency and the reporting officer (and, if she appeared, of the evidence of the mother herself), whether it had sufficient information on which to accept the mother's decision to relinquish parental rights and obligations. If not, it would be open to the court to call for further information from the agency, or from the reporting officer, or to require the mother to attend. Until experience of the new procedure has been gained, we envisage that the courts would require the agency's representative or the reporting officer to be present.

181. It would be open to the mother to withdraw her application at any time before the court hearing. The procedure we recommend in paragraph 179 should make it possible for the court hearing to take place shortly after the mother had signed the form in the presence of the reporting officer.

182. The relinquishment procedure could not be completed before a child was six weeks old, but we do not think that placement of the child with prospective adopters should necessarily be delayed until it had been completed. Where the agency is of the opinion that the mother is unlikely to change her preliminary decision to relinquish parental rights, the child might well be placed at an earlier stage, e.g. direct from hospital. This would make it possible to tell the mother about the prospective adopters, even though she had relinquished her parental rights. We appreciate that most mothers want to know something of the family chosen for their child, but we think that, even when relinquishment took place before placement, agencies would usually be able to tell the mother about the family with whom they planned to place her child and, if the mother wished, they would be able to give further details during any follow-up work with the mother.

183. But there might still be some mothers who would wish to retain their

parental rights until an adoption order had been made. We consider that the relinquishment procedure should be an option open to the mother, and research suggests that many would prefer to give an early, final consent and would be likely to use it. Mothers wishing to place their child for adoption would therefore be given a choice between the new relinquishment procedure and consent to adoption by specific adopters which would not become final until the adoption order was made. We suggest that this choice should be explained in a leaflet describing the two procedures, which would be given to the mother who should acknowledge that she has read it and had it explained to her. A possible outline of such a leaflet is given at Appendix E.

Should the mother be approached if her child is not adopted after relinquishment?

184. An agency would be unlikely to support an application for relinquishment unless it was reasonably confident that it could find an adoptive home for the child. If placement seemed likely to be difficult, the agency would be likely to defer the relinquishment application until a placement had been effected or was assured. In the rare case where relinquishment had taken place and adoption proved impossible, the agency would retain parental rights and obligations. We suggested in our working paper that it would not be right for the agency to make a further approach to the mother in these circumstances, but in the light of the evidence we received, most of which was in favour of enabling the mother to be approached if she wished, we recommend that the mother should be able to resume care of the child, if she wished to do so, and that it should be possible for her in suitable cases to resume parental rights and obligations. Such a restoration of parental rights would have to be carefully defined, otherwise the irrevocability of relinquishment would be prejudiced in order to deal with a few highly exceptional cases. A possible method would be to give the mother the right to apply to the court for parental rights and obligations to be re-vested in her if an adoption order had not been made within twelve months of the relinquishment hearing. This right would not be exercisable if an adoption application were before the court. To make this right effective it would be necessary to place a duty on the agency to notify the mother if the child had not been adopted within twelve months (without prejudice to the discretion of the agency to tell her, at an earlier stage, that adoption was unlikely). If the mother did not wish to be re-involved in this way she would have an opportunity to sign a statement to this effect before the reporting officer.

185. We think that, in practice, cases in which this provision could be used would be rare. When they arose, it would be possible for the mother to resume *de facto* the custody of the child at an earlier stage without any statutory provisions of this kind. But we recognise the force of the argument that she should also be able to resume the legal rights and obligations of a parent, and we recommend that the law should provide for their resumption in the way outlined in paragraph 184.

Timing of the change in the law introducing relinquishment

186. For the relinquishment procedure to be operated it is essential that adoption agencies should be in a position to exercise parental rights over a

child in the interval between relinquishment and adoption. We recommend that this change in the law should not operate until after the new registration system has come into force and agencies have been registered under the new procedure.

Consent to adoption where the relinquishment procedure is not used

187. Clearly the relinquishment procedure could be used only where an adoption agency was involved. It could not be used where, for example, the applicant was a relative. We hope that the advantages of the relinquishment procedure would lead to its use in the great majority of agency cases, but there would probably be a number of instances where the mother wished to give consent to a specific application to adopt. In these cases, the existing law, under which parental rights and obligations are not transferred until an adoption order is made, would continue to apply. In cases of dispute, any application to dispense with consent would be heard by the court hearing the adoption application. Consent could be given at the hearing of the application and, as at present, it would be open to the mother to provide written evidence of her consent. We recommend that the procedure for providing such evidence should be similar to that which we have recommended in paragraphs 176 and 177 for relinquishment applications. The applicants would notify the court of their intention to apply for an adoption order and the court would appoint a reporting officer. If the mother gave a written consent, witnessed by the reporting officer, the applicants would attach it to their application together with a report from the reporting officer. As at present, the mother would not be entitled to remove the child from the care of the applicants without the leave of the court.

Timing of the mother's consent

188. Under the present law a mother's consent to adoption is not valid unless given at least six weeks after the birth of the child; this delay is intended to ensure that she has recovered from the effects of child-birth. We suggested in our working paper that this might be reduced to four weeks.

189. There was a wide divergence of views among our witnesses about the appropriate time, ranging from as soon as possible to three months. The majority appeared to favour four weeks, and we have already referred to research which showed that mothers generally thought that the consent procedure should be speeded up.[5]

190. Paragraph 4 of Article 5 of the European Convention on the Adoption of Children, which the United Kingdom has ratified, is in the following terms:

"4. A mother's consent to the adoption of her child shall not be accepted unless it is given at such time after the birth of the child, not being less than six weeks, as may be prescribed by law, or, if no such time has been prescribed, at such time as, in the opinion of the competent authority, will have enabled her to recover sufficiently from the effects of giving birth to the child."

It would appear possible for British law to prescribe no period, while complying with the convention, but not to prescribe four weeks. We think that the

54

convention might be more flexible on this point, but amendment might take some time, even if acceptable to other countries. The recommendations we make earlier in this chapter are designed to enable relinquishment proceedings to take place shortly after the child is six weeks old where the mother so wishes.

Recommendations

191. The law should enable parental rights to be relinquished and transferred to an adoption agency with a view to the child's adoption. Accordingly *we recommend* that:—

Relinquishment and transfer of parental rights should require the approval of a court, on an application made jointly by the parent and an adoption agency.

(Recommendation 37)

The court should be required to be satisfied that the mother, after considering the alternatives and implications, had freely decided to relinquish parental rights.

(Recommendation 38)

The court hearing a relinquishment application should have power to proceed in the absence of the mother and accept written evidence of her decision to relinquish parental rights.

(Recommendation 39)

Written evidence of her decision should be witnessed by a social worker appointed by the court, known as the reporting officer, who would have a duty to furnish the court with a report on whether the mother had freely made her decision after considering the alternatives and implications.

(Recommendation 40)

The rights and interests of any other person or body (e.g. a putative father or a local authority having care of the child) should be considered before an order transferring parental rights was made.

(Recommendation 41)

If satisfied that the mother had freely decided to relinquish parental rights, with a full understanding of its implications and the alternatives, the court should make an order vesting all parental rights in the agency, which would retain them until an adoption order was made.

(Recommendation 42)

The transfer of parental rights should be irrevocable, subject to the right of the mother to ask to be notified if no adoption order was made within twelve months and, in that case, to apply to the court for parental rights to be restored, unless an adoption application was then before the court. If no such application was made by the mother the agency would retain the rights and obligations until the child's majority or until they were transferred by court order, or transferred to some other local authority or agency by agreement approved by the court.

(Recommendation 43)

The agency to which parental rights had been transferred should have the power to consent to an adoption order on producing the order of the court which had transferred parental rights.

(Recommendation 44)

Consent to a specific adoption application should become final, as at present, when an adoption order was made, the mother being a respondent to the adoption application. A reporting officer would be appointed, who would witness the mother's written consent and make a report to the court.

(Recommendation 45)

The period before which the mother cannot give consent to adoption should remain six weeks so long as the European Convention on Adoption so provides. The same minimum period should apply to the written statement of willingness to relinquish parental rights made before the reporting officer.

(Recommendation 46)

The putative father

192. The consent of the natural father to the making of an adoption order in respect of his illegitimate child is not required because the courts have held that he is not a parent for the purpose of section 5 of the 1958 Act.* We think the opportunity should be taken to embody this decision in the statute law. If, however, he is "liable by virtue of an order or agreement to contribute to the maintenance of the infant", he must, under rules of court, be made a respondent to the application and receive a notice of the hearing. Even if this does not apply, he may be made a respondent if the court considers him to be a person who ought to receive notice of the hearing. In England and Wales, the guardian ad litem has a duty to inform the court if he learns of any person claiming to be the father who wishes to be heard by the court on the question whether an adoption order should be made (Second Schedule to the Adoption (Court) Rules).†

193. In England and Wales, section 14 of the Guardianship of Minors Act 1971 entitles the father of an illegitimate child to apply under section 9 of that Act for the custody of the child. In Scotland, the father may apply for custody under the Illegitimate Children (Scotland) Act 1930. We think that the putative father's right to apply for custody should remain.

194. The attitude of putative fathers varies widely from those who have no interest whatsoever in the child, to those who have been living with the mother in what has been a stable union and regard the child as just as much their responsibility as if he had been born to them in wedlock. It is important that the putative father's interests should be considered at an early stage. If a mother seeks to relinquish her parental rights with a view to the child's adoption, a putative father who has contributed to the child's maintenance, or is actively involved in helping the mother, or interested in the child and his future, should be made a respondent to the relinquishment application. If he wished to apply for guardianship it would be desirable that the application should be dealt with by the court which hears the relinquishment application. (This would become possible in magistrates' courts in England and Wales as a result

---

* See *Re M* (an infant) [1957] 2 All ER 911 [1955] 2 QB 479 (England and Wales) and *A v B* 1955 SC 378 (Scotland).
† In Scotland, the Act of Sederunt stipulates that the curator must inform the court of any other person who should be given notice. The putative father is not specifically mentioned.

of our recommendation that adoption jurisdiction should be transferred from juvenile courts to domestic courts—see paragraph 263).

195. Some mothers are unwilling to identify the father, and they cannot be made to do so; some do not know who he is, and there are some men who are unwilling to be involved. The first responsibility for ascertaining the position rests with the agency, and in the report which accompanies a relinquishment application the agency should describe the situation fully, so that the court may decide whether to notify the putative father of the proceedings. If the reporting officer is the first to learn of information about the putative father, or obtains further information which is not in the agency report, he should include it in his report to the court. It would be good practice for him to let the agency also know what he has learned.

196. In view of the need to ensure that the result of relinquishment proceedings will be an unchallengeable transfer of parental rights, it is important that the putative father should be notified of the proceedings where he is known and can be found. If the putative father does not appear, the court will need to be satisfied that he does not wish to, or that the agency has made reasonable efforts to trace him without success. If he is known and can be found, the reporting officer should ascertain whether he wishes to attend the court. If he does not, he should be invited to sign a statement to that effect, which the reporting officer would forward to the court. But if the father's identity is not established, or he cannot be found after genuine enquiry, or he fails to appear, this should not prevent the court from transferring parental rights with a view to adoption. Once this is done, the rights and obligations of the putative father should be terminated, in the same way that they are now terminated by an adoption order, including any obligation to pay maintenance under an affiliation order, or a decree of affiliation and aliment, or an agreement.

197. In the case of applications for adoption by relatives and foster parents there will be no reinquishment hearing, and the putative father's position will still have to be considered as part of the adoption proceedings. It will still be desirable for his position to be considered at an early stage and the local authority should see that the necessary enquiries are made.

Recommendations

198. Normally the involvement of a putative father in planning for a child's future should be encouraged. Accordingly *we recommend* that:—

The putative father's right to apply for custody should remain.

(Recommendation 47)

In relinquishment proceedings the putative father's interests should be finally determined at that stage; if he has been concerned in the child's upbringing and maintenance he should be made a respondent to a relinquishment application; but if he is not known, cannot be found or fails to appear, then freeing of the child for adoption should not be delayed.

(Recommendation 48)

Once parental rights have been transferred to an agency the right of the putative father to apply for custody should be terminated, together with his obligation to pay maintenance under an affiliation order, or decree of affiliation and aliment, or an agreement.

(Recommendation 49)

The mother's husband

199. A child born within wedlock is presumed legitimate and the consent of both parents is required to any adoption application. Difficulties often arise in the case of extra-marital children, and much distress can be caused through the disclosure to the husband of the existence of an illegitimate child. Such a disclosure is pointless and unreasonable where a couple have lived apart for many years.

200. Many courts accept evidence presented by the mother of non-access, e.g. where a separation order is in force, or where a mother has sworn an affidavit about non-access, or gives evidence of it in person. Other courts insist in all cases on the consent of the husband, and we have been told that some consider it their duty to inform a husband of his wife's adultery; we think these practices should cease.

201. Where there is an application for relinquishment the position of the mother's husband must be considered at that stage. Unless it is established that he is not a parent he must join in the application for relinquishment. There was some difference of opinion among our witnesses as to what evidence should be required to establish that a mother's husband is not the father of the child. It was pointed out that it may be dangerous to allow a mother to bastardise her child without supporting evidence; on the other hand, a husband can be obstructive by making a false claim to paternity.

202. We consider that where, in relinquishment proceedings, a mother wishes to adduce evidence that her husband is not the father of the child, the agency should say so in its report, but the court should not inform the husband of the relinquishment application at that stage. We suggest that the better course would be for the court to ask the mother to attend the relinquishment hearing, when the court could consider, on the basis of the evidence before it, whether it was satisfied that the husband was not the father of the child and need not be involved because he was not a parent. It may be that a court would rarely be satisfied on this point if the evidence did not also include independent evidence other than that given by the mother herself. In some cases blood tests might be ordered to assist in establishing paternity.* If the court were not so satisfied, on the balance of probabilities, it would have to refuse the application because one of the child's parents was not a party to it. If the mother's husband claimed paternity and agreed that the child should be adopted, a fresh application by both parents and the agency could be made. If the father did not agree to join in the application it would be possible, on a specific adoption application being made, or on an application to free the child for adoption (see paragraphs 221 to 225), to ask a court to dispense with his consent to adoption.

---

* Under section 20(1) of the Family Law Reform Act 1969 in England and Wales. There is no corresponding power in Scotland to order blood tests.

Recommendation

203. *We recommend* that:—

Where there is a relinquishment application the position of the mother's husband should be considered at that stage. If the mother states that her husband is not the father, the court should not notify the husband of the relinquishment application until it has heard any evidence brought on behalf of the mother to support her statement. If the mother fails to satisfy the court that her husband is not the father, yet wishes to continue with the application, she should be informed that the proceedings cannot continue unless the husband joins her as an applicant.

(Recommendation 50)

Dispensing with consent to an adoption application

204. One of the main objects of our recommendations is to reduce as far as possible the number of cases in which conflicts arise. The new relinquishment procedure will enable the natural parent to give up parental rights earlier in the child's life and so reduce the situations, which sometimes arise under the existing law, where a mother changes her mind after the child has been placed with adopters for some months.* Nevertheless, there will inevitably be some conflict situations in which the court will have to consider whether to dispense with consent.

The welfare of the child

205. The 1958 Act (section 5) gives the court power to dispense with consent if it is satisfied that the person whose consent is to be dispensed with

(a) has abandoned, neglected or persistently ill-treated the infant; or

(b) cannot be found or is incapable of giving his consent; or

(c) has persistently failed without reasonable cause to discharge the obligations of a parent or guardian of the infant; or

(d) is withholding his consent unreasonably.

206. The section makes no express reference to the welfare of the child. Although section 7 of the 1958 Act requires the court to be satisfied that an adoption order will be for the welfare of the child, the question of consent has to be dealt with before that stage is reached. Yet the decision whether to dispense with consent may be as important to the child as a decision whether to make an adoption order.

207. The law on custody disputes between parents (section 1 of the Guardianship of Minors Act 1971, which consolidates the earlier law)† requires the court to "regard the welfare of the minor as the first and paramount consideration" and prohibits it from taking into consideration from any other point of view the superiority of the claim of the father or the mother.

208. Many adoption workers were concerned about the fact that adoption

---

* The Survey of Adoption in Great Britain[1] found that in 15 (or 0·5 per cent) of the cases in their sample the mother withdrew her consent after the adoption application had been sent to the court.

† In Scotland, section 1 of the Guardianship of Infants Act, 1925.

law did not make the welfare of the child paramount, or even as important as the rights of the parents. In our working paper we suggested the possible application to adoption law of the principle that the welfare of the child should be the first and paramount consideration. At the same time we thought it right to suggest the retention of the principle that adoption should normally be possible only with parental consent, although it should be open to a court to dispense with that consent on certain specified grounds. We suggested the retention, with some minor modifications, of the existing grounds set out in paragraph 205. In so far as those grounds which depend on the reasonableness of the natural parent might conflict with the principle that the welfare of the child should be paramount, we suggested that the interpretation of what was reasonable or unreasonable should be subject to that principle.

209. The great majority of witnesses supported the general principle, although some sounded a note of caution. A number gave their support on the assumption that the courts would recognise that the child's welfare included maintaining links with natural parents where this was in the child's interests. Some criticisms of our proposal may be summed up by the statement of more than one witness that it depended on what was meant by welfare. Some feared that the law would be weighted too heavily against the natural parents; and that, in forming a view on welfare, courts might place too much emphasis on wealth and social status.

210. There was less comment on how the principle might be applied to the law on dispensing with consent. In our working paper we explained that "as the law on dispensing with consents now stands the courts will not necessarily consider a parent to be unreasonable in withholding consent, or withdrawing it once given, even if in the particular case it seems to be against the welfare of the child that the parent should remain responsible for him". This reflected our anxiety about two conflicting lines of judicial decisions, one of which interpreted unreasonableness as necessarily involving a degree of culpability. Since our working paper was prepared, this conflict of judicial opinion has been resolved by the House of Lords in the case of *Re W*.*

211. In that case (in which the decision of the county court judge to dispense with the mother's consent was upheld), the House of Lords held that it was not necessary to show a degree of culpability on the part of the parent before it could be established that she was withholding consent unreasonably. They approved the following passage from a judgment of Lord Denning in an earlier case which, the Lord Chancellor said, could now be considered authoritative.

> "In considering the matter I quite agree that: (1) the question whether she is unreasonably withholding her consent is to be judged at the date of the hearing; and (2) the welfare of the child is not the sole consideration; and (3) the one question is whether she is unreasonably withholding her consent. But I must say that in considering whether she is reasonable or unreasonable we must take into account the welfare of the child. A reasonable mother surely gives great weight to what is better

* *Re W* [1971] 2 All ER 49.

for the child. Her anguish of mind is quite understandable; but still it may be unreasonable for her to withhold consent. We must look and see whether it is reasonable or unreasonable according to what a reasonable woman in her place would do in all the circumstances of the case."*

The decision in Re W has clarified the law by establishing that the welfare of the child is to be taken into account in deciding whether the mother is acting unreasonably in withholding her consent to adoption. This was one of the objects of the suggestion in our working paper. In the light of this clarification, which we welcome, we have re-considered our suggestion that in deciding whether the mother is unreasonable, the interpretation of what is unreasonable should be subject to the principle that the child's welfare should be the first and paramount consideration.

212. We have come to the conclusion that, if the child's welfare were declared to be paramount, the test of whether the mother was withholding consent unreasonably could not remain. The choice, therefore, appears to lie between two approaches. The first approach is along the lines of the House of Lords' decision in Re W, retaining the existing grounds for dispensing with consent but taking account of the long-term welfare of the child in deciding whether the mother is acting unreasonably. The second approach would be to abandon the existing grounds for dispensing with consent, including the unreasonableness test, and to give the courts a general power to dispense with parental consent to adoption if they were satisfied that to do so would be for the long-term welfare of the child, this being the first and paramount consideration.

213. The words "the first and paramount consideration" were used by Parliament in 1925 in order to make it clear beyond doubt that, in disputes between parents over the custody of their children, the two parties were to be on an equal footing, with no presumption in favour of one or the other. The parties to the proceedings are the child's parents and a custody order in favour of either may be varied by the courts in the light of changed circumstances.

214. In adoption, on the other hand, where the order is final and irrevocable and involves the transfer of parental rights to strangers, the law has given weight to the wishes of the mother, provided she does not act unreasonably.

215. Our witnesses were unanimous about the need for the child's welfare to be taken fully into account when the court is deciding whether to dispense with consent. The question is whether it should be made the paramount consideration. We think that the court has to take account of a number of factors and that Lord Reid described the reality of the situation in the case of O'Connor v A and B† when he said:

"The test is an objective test—would a reasonable parent have withheld consent? I think that a reasonable parent or, indeed, any other reasonable

---

* Re L, Times Law Report, 19 July 1962.
† [1971] 1 WLR 1227. This was another case in which a decision to dispense with consent was upheld. The italics in the extract are ours.

person, would have in mind the interests or claims of all three parties concerned—the child whose adoption is in question, the natural parents, and the adopting family. *No doubt the child's interests come first* and in some cases they may be paramount. But I see no reason why the claims of the natural parents should be ignored. If the mother were deeply attached to the child and had only consented in the first place to adoption because of adverse circumstances it would seem to me unjust that on a change of circumstances her affection for the child and her natural claim as a parent should be ignored. And the adopting family cannot be ignored either. If it was the mother's action that brought them in, in the first place, they ought not to be displaced without good reason. So to balance these claims is no easy task. Often no ideal solution is possible. We are dealing largely with future probabilities for the decision once made is irrevocable. So we cannot be certain what will be in the child's best interests in the long run. That seems to me to be an additional reason for giving considerable weight in proper cases to the claims of the natural parents and of the adopting family."

Child's welfare as the first consideration

216. We think that the law should recognise that there are a number of interests to be considered and put the interests of the child first among them. It seems to us that the objective reasonableness of the mother is an appropriate test, and that in deciding whether she is withholding consent unreasonably the court should take account of all the circumstances, first consideration being given to the effect of her decision on the long-term welfare of the child.

217. It was argued by some witnesses that the recent decision of the House of Lords had at last established a body of settled law and that, since any change we might propose could lead to another period of uncertainty, the law should be left alone. We do not accept this argument. We think the welfare of the child is of such importance that the duty of the court to give it first consideration should be embodied in the statute law.

Recommendation

218. *We therefore recommend* that:—

The statute law should provide that, in deciding whether a parent is withholding consent to adoption unreasonably, the court shall have regard to all the circumstances, first consideration being given to the effect of the parent's decision on the long-term welfare of the child.

(Recommendation 51)

Other changes in the grounds for dispensing with consent

219. We suggested in our working paper that the first ground set out in paragraph 205 should be amended so as to include persistent or *serious* ill-treatment. Our witnesses were divided, some arguing that a single case of serious ill-treatment should not be a ground for dispensing with consent. We are aware of the fact that rehabilitation of an injured child with his family is often possible, and had in mind serious ill-treatment in circumstances which made such rehabilitation unlikely.

Recommendation

220. We think this consideration should be embodied in the law and *we recommend* that:—

An additional ground on which the court should be empowered to dispense with the consent of a parent to adoption should be that the parent has seriously ill-treated the child and the court is satisfied that the rehabilitation of the child in the family is unlikely.

(Recommendation 52)

Agency applications to dispense with consent

221. There is known to exist a sizeable number of children in the care of local authorities and voluntary societies for whom no permanent future can be arranged for a variety of reasons, for example, because the parents cannot bring themselves to make a plan, or do not want their child adopted but are unable to look after him themselves. Some of these children may have no contact with their parents and would benefit from adoption, but the parents will not agree to it. In other cases a parent may have her child received into care shortly after birth and then vacillate for months or even years over the question of adoption, thus depriving her child of the security of a settled family home life.

222. Information received from Dr Barbara Tizard, who is carrying out research on the development of children who spent their earliest years in a residential nursery, has identified a group of such children in the care of voluntary societies in a particular year. The records of Dr Barnardo's, the Church of England Children's Society and the National Children's Home were searched for children who reached the age of $4\frac{1}{2}$ during 1971, who had been full-term healthy babies, who had been admitted to a residential nursery in the first six months of life, and who had remained there without a break ever since. There were 25 such children, and in 17 of these cases the children were still in residential care because the mother had refused permission for adoption. Dr Tizard writes: "In these cases, some kind of contact, usually very intermittent, had been retained with one or other parent who declared that their eventual hope was to have the child back . . ."

223. In some of these cases a court might well consider that there were statutory grounds for dispensing with the parents' consent because they had persistently failed to discharge the obligations of a parent, or were withholding consent unreasonably. Under the present law there is no way of testing this without first placing the child with prospective adopters and awaiting a court decision after at least three months care and possession by them. If the court then decides that there are insufficient grounds for dispensing with the parents' consent the child must be returned to the agency. Moreover, unless the child is in the care of a local authority which has parental rights, or a care order has been made, the parents can frustrate the proceedings by removing the child before the court hearing. Agencies are therefore understandably reluctant to place these children for adoption.

224. We accept the principle that the natural family should be preserved wherever reasonably possible. But where a child is in care with no satisfactory

long-term plan in mind, and lacking the possibility of long-term stable relationships, we think that it should be open to a local authority or a registered adoption agency to apply to a court for the parents' consent to be dispensed with on one of the statutory grounds, for parental rights to be transferred to the agency and the child thus freed for placement for adoption. The parents should not be permitted to remove the child from the agency's care without the leave of the court while the application is pending. This procedure would enable a decision to be taken without a child first being placed for adoption. The hearing would be in the nature of a relinquishment hearing but with the application made by the local authority or agency. Such an application would be made only where there was every prospect of a satisfactory placement for the child, and if it were granted the agency would have parental rights and obligations until an adoption order was made.

Recommendation

225. *We recommend* that:—

The law should enable a local authority or registered adoption society to apply to a court for the transfer of parental rights over a child in their care to the agency with a view to the child's adoption and for the parents' consent to adoption to be dispensed with on one of the statutory grounds. The law should prevent the removal of the child by a parent pending the hearing.

(Recommendation 53)

*Procedure where there is an application
to dispense with consent*

226. In *Re M** Lord Justice Sachs suggested that differences between the High Court Rules and the County Court Rules merited our urgent attention and that of the County Court Rules Committee. A complete revision of all the court rules will be necessary following the legislation which, we hope, will implement the recommendations made earlier in this chapter, and we did not consider that it would be useful for us, at a late stage in our work, to embark on a detailed study of rules of court. There is, however, one point, which was dealt with in *Re M,* which we think merits urgent attention. We consider that where applicants for an adoption order intend to ask that parental consent should be dispensed with, the parent and the court should be furnished, in advance of the hearing, with particulars of the matters on which they intend to rely. The Court of Appeal has already directed that this should be done in relation to applications on the ground that consent is unreasonably withheld† and the High Court Rules now require it in all cases.

Recommendation

227. Accordingly *we recommend* that:—

Rules of court should require a person who intends to ask any court to dispense with a parent's consent to adoption to furnish the court, and the parent, in advance of the hearing, with a statement of the matters on which he intends to rely.

(Recommendation 54)

---

* *Re M,* Times Law Report, 2 May 1972.
† *Re W* [1970] 3 All ER 990 at page 997. The Court of Appeal decision was reversed by the House of Lords on grounds unconnected with this point.

Consent subject to a condition
as to religious upbringing

228. Consent to the making of an adoption order can at present be given subject to a condition with respect to the religious persuasion in which the infant is proposed to be brought up (section 4(2) of the Adoption Act 1958). When adoption law was last reviewed "religious persuasion" in this country was likely to mean a particular denomination of the Christian church, or the Jewish religion. There are now many more mothers of other faiths, some from overseas.

229. The arguments which were put to us against the retention of this condition are:

(a) that if adoption is the complete severance of the legal relationship between parents and child (see paragraph 14) it is anomalous that the parent should appear to retain control over this one aspect of the child's future;

(b) that the condition is unenforceable and might bring the law into disrepute. By "unenforceable" is meant that there is no way in which the adoptive parents can be made to carry out their promise to bring the child up in a particular religious persuasion or be made to try to do so;

(c) that it may be contrary to the best interests of the child in that adopters may be selected not because they are the most suitable but because there is a shortage of adopters of the religious persuasion named by the mother, or there may be considerable delay in placement while adopters of a particular sect are sought.

230. We therefore proposed in our working paper that it should no longer remain possible for the mother to make her consent conditional in this way. We expected that the agency, whether or not it had any religious affiliations, would ascertain whether the mother had any wishes in the matter of religious upbringing and, if she had, would have regard to those wishes when selecting adopters. If, however, it was impracticable to comply with the wish expressed by the mother, or to do so might be harmful to the child's welfare (e.g. because it might involve undue delay), we suggested that the agency should be free to make whatever placement appeared to be in the best interests of the child. It would remain open to a mother of a particular religious persuasion to go to a voluntary society which serves those of her faith in the expectation that the child would be adopted by those of similar beliefs.

Recommendation

231. The majority of witnesses supported this suggestion although some, but not all, Roman Catholic witnesses opposed it. *We recommend* that:—

It should cease to be possible to give consent to adoption subject to a condition as to the religious persuasion in which the child is to be brought up.

(Recommendation 55)

CHAPTER 9

ADOPTION PROCEDURE

The making of adoption orders

232. We suggested in our working paper that, because adoption involved a permanent change in the legal relationship between the child, his natural parents and the adopters, the use of judicial process was an essential safeguard to protect the rights and interests of the people involved and especially of the child, and for the resolution of conflicts when these arose. It was necessary also for decisions on questions of eligibility, which might, for instance, raise difficult legal problems about domicile. There was virtually complete agreement with this view among our witnesses and we recommend that decisions on the granting or refusal of adoption orders should continue to be taken by courts.

The present procedure

233. In agency cases the procedure starts with the social work service given by the agency to natural parents, adopters and child, leading up to the placing of the child with the applicants. The agency must supervise the child in the home until the adopters notify the local authority of their intention to apply for an adoption order. In good agency practice, the agency social worker retains contact with the natural parents, with the child and with the prospective adopters at least until the order has been made.

234. Section 3 of the 1958 Act contains two interlinked requirements which must be complied with before an adoption order is made. The first requires the applicants (unless one of them is a parent of the child or the child is above the upper limit of compulsory school age) to notify the local authority, at least three months before the date of the order, of their intention to apply for an adoption order. The local authority supervises the child in the home, and this supervision is called "welfare supervision". The second requires the child to have been continuously in the care and possession of the applicants for at least three consecutive months immediately preceding the date of the order, not counting the first six weeks of the child's life. The purpose of this second requirement is to allow a period for the child to settle in the home and for the applicants to adapt to their new role as parents, before the court considers the application. This three months' period largely overlaps the period of welfare supervision and the role of the welfare supervisor is to watch over the child's well-being and to assist the settling-in process.

235. Meanwhile, the applicants complete their applications and file it with the court. The application papers include medical report forms, and the documents signifying the consent of the natural parents. The court appoints a guardian ad litem, fixes a time for the hearing of the application and serves the requisite notices on the natural parents and on anyone else with a claim to be heard (the "respondents"). The guardian ad litem interviews the applicants as part of his enquiries and makes a confidential report to the court. The actual hearing is attended by the applicants, by the guardian and usually

by the child.* The respondents may also appear and be heard, though proceedings must be conducted in such a way as to safeguard confidentiality in cases where the proposed adopters have applied under a serial number.

236. There is dissatisfaction with the existing procedure because in agency cases the parents and adopters are involved with at least two different social workers† (the agency worker and the guardian ad litem) and sometimes with three (where the welfare supervisor and the guardian are different officers), as well as the health visitor. The enquiries of the guardian ad litem duplicate those of the agency. Adoptive parents are bewildered by these different workers and often fail to distinguish between them or to understand their respective functions. This duplication of visiting, it has been suggested, is a wasteful and ineffectual use of scarce social work resources.

Welfare supervision

237. We are in no doubt about the need for a settling-in period, and a period of supervision and help. This was introduced in 1949 and its value is well established. The Guide to Adoption Practice[3] describes the aim of welfare supervision as being "to offer a supporting service to adopters, help them to focus on the essential task of integrating the child into their family life, and look forward confidently to the future. The welfare supervisor . . . should concentrate on the particular needs of this period: the adoptive parents' pre-occupation with the physical care of the child, their adaptation to new family roles and changed relationships". We are convinced that this kind of help can best be offered by the agency responsible for choosing the adoptive home and placing the child. The agency is in the best position to help the couple to adapt to their new role and to deal with any problems they may have. For this reason we suggested in our working paper that welfare supervision by the local authority might be abolished in agency cases and full responsibility for the protection of the child, and for supervising and advising the adopters, should be placed upon the agency alone. This would make a better use of social work resources and also provide a better service to the adoptive family and to the court. As a consequence, it would no longer be necessary, in agency cases, for the applicants to notify the local authority of their intention to apply to the court for an adoption order.

238. Although some witnesses feared that agency standards were not good enough, there was a large measure of agreement with our suggestion. We recommend therefore that in agency cases, once the new registration procedure is in force, welfare supervision by the local authority should not be required and the statutory responsibility for supervising the child in the adoptive home should rest with the placing agency throughout the period between the placement and the court hearing. The capacity of an agency to undertake this work would be among the factors considered when an agency applied for registration (see Appendix C(j)).

239. The placing agency should be able to delegate supervision to another

---

* In Scotland the holding of hearings is subject to the discretion of the court, and they are infrequent except in contested cases.
† In Scotland it may be a social worker and a solicitor, the latter acting as curator ad litem.

agency or to the local authority (for example where the applicants move to another part of the country), but the placing agency should retain the statutory responsibility for the case.

240. In non-agency cases (applications by relatives and foster parents) the existing requirement to notify the local authority of intention to apply for an adoption order should continue. The local authority should carry out certain of the functions which would otherwise have fallen to the placing agency, that is, full enquiries into and assessment of the situation, supervision and protection of the child in the home, help and support to the applicants and the preparation of a report for the court.

The care and possession period

241. There was a large measure of agreement with the suggestion in our working paper that the care and possession period should remain three months, although it was recognised that this should be seen as a minimum period. We recommend that the statutory period should remain three months, the first six weeks of the child's life as at present not counting towards this period.

242. Too restrictive an interpretation of "three months' care and possession" can make compliance with this requirement very difficult where, for example, a child is at a special school and only at home during the holidays. We doubt, however, whether it is necessary to change the law to cover cases of this kind. The High Court has not required continuous physical possession by applicants who have been in effective control of the child.*

243. Section 12 of the 1958 Act provides that applicants who are domiciled here but resident abroad are deemed to have fulfilled the requirements if one applicant has had care and possession for at least three consecutive months and both applicants have lived together in this country for one of those months. Problems have arisen in the past when the one month of joint care and possession falls at the beginning of the period of care and possession. Unless the court hearing follows immediately at the end of the three months, the one month will not come within the three months immediately preceding the date of the order as required by section 3(1) of the 1958 Act. We recommend that the court should be given discretion in such cases.

Information to the court

244. There remains the question of accountability and reporting to the court. This is closely linked with the function of the guardian ad litem. At present, the placing agency and the local authority responsible for welfare supervision do not report direct to the court. In England and Wales, it is the duty of the guardian ad litem to "obtain from every respondent, not being an individual, such information concerning the infant as they have in their possession, and which they consider might assist the court in deciding whether or not the infant should be adopted by the applicants. Where such information is given in the form of a written report, the guardian ad litem shall append it to his

---

* *Re B* (An infant) [1963] 3 All ER 125.

own report to the court".* We consider that the law ought to recognise the decisive part played by the agency in arranging the adoption by making the agency accountable to the court. The court will have to make judgments on assessments and decisions made by the agency. It ought to have a first hand account of them and the opportunity to question the agency about them. The agency should therefore make a comprehensive report to the court and should have the opportunity of explaining to the court the reasons for that particular placement. It follows that the agency should be represented at the hearing by a social worker able to speak to the report. This would not preclude the agency from having legal representation where it considered this appropriate.

The guardian ad litem†—the present position

245. The present law requires the court to appoint a guardian ad litem in all adoption applications. The appointment is made soon after the adoption application has been lodged with the court. The guardian's primary duty is to safeguard the interests of the child before the court. In addition he has to investigate all circumstances relevant to the proposed adoption. This includes verifying the statements contained in the application, ascertaining that consents have been freely given, and helping to ensure that anyone who has a right to be heard has the opportunity. His duties are set out in considerable detail in the Court Rules in England and Wales and by Act of Sederunt in Scotland. His enquiries have to cover a number of matters of fact, as well as more intangible aspects of personality and understanding, to enable him to make an assessment as to whether adoption would be for the child's welfare. In England and Wales, the guardian is normally the Director of Social Services or a member of his staff, or a probation officer, though in the High Court the Official Solicitor carries out these duties. In Scotland the court may appoint either a solicitor or a social worker.

Mandatory or discretionary appointment

246. In the light of the criticism of the present system referred to in paragraph 236, we suggested in our working paper that the appointment of the guardian should no longer be mandatory but should be at the discretion of the court. We made suggestions about the way he should carry out his functions, for instance, by making enquiries initially of the agency, by concentrating on certain areas of enquiry as directed by the court, and interviewing the parties concerned only where this was necessary to carry out the court's instructions. We suggested also that his duties should always be carried out by social workers. These suggestions were closely linked with the suggestion that adoption agencies should supervise the child in the adoptive home throughout the care and possession period and until the court hearing, and should report direct to the court and be represented at the hearing.

247. There was a considerable amount of comment on the suggestion that the appointment of the guardian should be discretionary, and the evidence presented widely conflicting views. Generally speaking, agreement came mostly

---

* Adoption (County Court) Rules, Second Schedule, and corresponding High Court and juvenile court Rules.

† In the following paragraphs the term "guardian" is used instead of guardian ad litem, and includes a curator ad litem in Scotland.

from professional social work agencies, especially those involved in adoption placement work. Some legal and medical associations also agreed. Disagreement focussed mainly on two aspects: doubts about present standards of practice of placing agencies; and the view that an independent and impartial investigation was necessary as a safeguard to all parties and primarily the child. In general, the evidence on this issue related to the existing procedures for adoption applications and the giving of consents, and not to the new procedures suggested in Chapter 8.

The guardian ad litem under our proposed new procedures

248. In view of our recommendations about relinquishment (see Chapter 8), it is appropriate to consider the question in relation to the three different situations in which the guardian might be involved

(a) a "relinquishment" application;

(b) an adoption application in cases where relinquishment has taken place; and

(c) an adoption application where relinquishment has not taken place.

249. Where there is a joint application, by the parent and agency, for the relinquishment of parental rights, we envisage that the court may wish to appoint a guardian if there are conflicts, for example between natural parents. Where the court, after considering the report from the reporting officer, is in doubt about whether the mother's decision to relinquish was freely made, it may wish to appoint a guardian. But there will be many cases in which the court is satisfied on this point after considering the reports made to it and will not wish any further enquiry to be made. Our conclusion is that the appointment of a guardian in relinquishment proceedings should be discretionary and not mandatory.

250. In the second kind of situation, where parental rights have been relinquished, the next stage of the court's involvement will be at the adoption application itself. This might well be before a different court, e.g. a mother might relinquish parental rights before a court in Birmingham where she lived, and the adoption application be made before a court in Oxfordshire, where the applicants lived. The court's duty is to satisfy itself that adoption by the particular couple would be for the child's welfare. We have recommended (paragraph 244) that it should have a full report from the agency, and there should be fewer situations where the appointment of a guardian would be necessary. Where the court decides to appoint one, his function would be primarily to report on the adoptive applicants and the child's well-being in the home.

251. The third kind of situation will be where parental rights have not been relinquished. In this kind of case proceedings will be similar to adoption applications under the present law. The court will have a report by the agency or, under the arrangements we have recommended in paragraph 240, from the local authority. Since, in these cases, the court has to consider a number of issues at the same hearing, the appointment of a guardian may more often be justified.

252. Our conclusion is that in all three situations the appointment of the guardian should be at the discretion of the court. Courts might regard some types of adoption application as requiring the automatic appointment of a guardian, for instance, where there is an application to dispense with consent. Agencies may often be able to advise the court about cases which might warrant the appointment of a guardian, thus reducing the risk of delay.

253. Where the court decides to appoint a guardian, it would be helpful if it would indicate the aspects of the case which give rise to concern or uncertainty and in respect of which it particularly needs help. We think it should be a matter of good practice for the guardian to make his enquiries of the agency or local authority in the first instance, so as to avoid unnecessary duplication of enquiries and to acquire an understanding of the background of the case.

254. We are of the opinion that, in the great majority of cases, the enquiries which the guardian is required to make are predominantly social enquiries, that social work skills are needed, and that social workers are the appropriate people to be appointed. Lawyers are able to satisfy themselves as to the legal aspects of the case, but are not generally equipped to make social assessments. We consider that the court should appoint the guardian from a panel of officers, approved by the court, comprising senior social workers drawn from the staffs of local authorities, the probation service, or other social work organisations in the area. The court should be precluded from appointing a guardian concerned with an agency or local authority involved in the case.

255. There may be contested cases in which it will be desirable for the guardian to have legal representation at the hearing. In many cases any legal issues will be fully argued by the representatives of the applicants or of the mother, but we consider that where the court is of the opinion that legal representation of the guardian is desirable it should have power to order the cost to be met from public funds.

256. Our recommendations about dispensing with welfare supervision by the local authority, about making the placing agency responsible for supervision and for reporting to the court, and about the discretionary appointment of guardians ad litem depend on the raising of standards of agency resources and practice. These additional responsibilities call for additional staff as well as a good standard of work to fulfil the aims of supervision. We recommend that these changes should not be brought into effect until the new registration arrangements recommended in Chapter 3 have been implemented.

Recommendations

257. *We recommend* that:—

Adoption orders should continue to be made by courts.

(Recommendation 56)

The agency which has placed the child should be responsible for the supervision of the child in the adoptive home, and for helping and advising the adopters throughout the period between the placement and the court hearing. Accordingly, welfare supervision of the child by the local authority, and the requirement to notify the local authority of the intention to apply for an adoption order, should be discontinued in agency cases once the new registration scheme has come into operation. The existing requirements for notification to the local authority and for welfare supervision should continue in non-agency cases.

(Recommendation 57)

The minimum period for which the applicants must have cared for the child before an adoption order can be granted should remain three months, not counting the first six weeks of the child's life.

(Recommendation 58)

Courts should have discretion to grant an order to joint applicants resident overseas where the period of care and possession in Great Britain by one of the applicants falls outside the three months immediately preceding the date of the order.

(Recommendation 59)

The agency should be accountable to the court, making a full written report direct to the court, being a party to the proceedings, and being represented at the hearing.

(Recommendation 60)

In both relinquishment and adoption applications the appointment of a guardian ad litem or curator ad litem should be at the discretion of the court.

(Recommendation 61)

The duties of a guardian or curator ad litem should be carried out by social workers, appointed from a list approved by the courts. The court should have discretion to order that the guardian should be legally represented at public expense.

(Recommendation 62)

None of the recommendations made in this chapter should be brought into force until the new registration procedure is in operation.

(Recommendation 63)

CHAPTER 10

THE COURT

258. England and Wales, and Scotland, have distinct and differing court systems. For convenience this Chapter is accordingly divided into two sections, one for England and Wales, and one for Scotland.

ENGLAND AND WALES

Courts having jurisdiction: the present position

259. In both adoption and guardianship, three courts have jurisdiction at first instance: the High Court, the county court and the magistrates' court. Few adoption orders* are made by the High Court each year and in practice adoption and guardianship jurisdiction at first instance is effectively shared between the county court and the magistrates' court. (International adoptions under the Hague Convention on Adoption[13] will, under the Adoption Act 1968, be heard only in the High Court; this is because such cases may involve complex issues of private international law. Provisional adoption orders, which are required if a person desires to remove a child from this country for adoption overseas, can be made only by the High Court or a county court, for similar reasons.)

260. For a considerable number of years magistrates' courts have been dealing with some 8,000* adoption applications a year. The county courts now deal with some 15,000* applications a year; this is a relatively recent development. In 1956 the county courts heard just over 5,000 applications and, as the total number of adoptions has increased, so has the proportion heard in the county courts. Some 80 per cent of adoptions granted by county courts are by non-relatives; and some 65 per cent of adoptions granted by magistrates' courts are by relatives. In guardianship, the position is reversed. Nearly all cases (some 6,000 a year) are heard in magistrates' courts,† and the county courts deal with fewer than 100 cases a year.

261. In order to give effect to the recommendations made earlier in our report, it is essential that the courts having jurisdiction to make adoption orders should also have jurisdiction to make guardianship orders. This is already the case in the High Court and the county court. In the magistrates' court, however, adoption applications are heard by the juvenile court, whose main business is dealing with children in need of care or control and prosecutions of children under 17. All the other family cases heard in magistrates' courts, including guardianship applications, are dealt with by the domestic court, i.e. the court which hears domestic cases (other than adoptions) as distinct from criminal and other non-domestic business. The juvenile court in each area is drawn from a special panel of magistrates selected for their suitability to deal

---

* See Appendix B, Table 1. Only 16 orders were made by the High Court in 1970.
† 6,312 applications were made to magistrates' courts in 1970 and they made 5,247 orders.

73

with cases involving children. All magistrates are eligible to sit in the domestic court.

262. For a number of years a "family court" to deal with family matters has been canvassed and the Law Commission has set up a Working Party with the following terms of reference:

"To consider, following the constitution of the Family Division of the High Court:—

(a) the structure, composition and jurisdiction of courts concerned with family matters below the level of the High Court, and

(b) what provision should be made for appeals from and transfers to and from these courts."

In this situation we think that the best course is for us first to set out the modifications to the existing system which, in our view, are necessary as a result of the recommendations made earlier in our report; and then to discuss the considerations which we consider relevant to family courts as far as adoption and guardianship are concerned.

Adoption proceedings in magistrates' courts

263. We have referred in paragraph 261 to the need to allocate adoption and guardianship applications to the same magistrates' court. Since all other family cases go to the domestic court it would be logical to transfer adoptions to that court. On the other hand, there are no special arrangements for ensuring that magistrates sitting in the domestic court are specially suited to this work. We recommend, as an interim measure, that adoption cases heard by magistrates should be transferred to the domestic court, and that arrangements should be made for selecting the magistrates who sit in this court, similar to those in force in respect of juvenile courts. The nature of family cases is such that those involved in them should not have to share waiting rooms and other court accommodation with people appearing in other kinds of case. When magistrates sit as a domestic court the law already requires that the sitting should so far as possible be held separately from other business. The aim should be, in all courts hearing adoption and guardianship cases, to hear these cases at different times from all other kinds of business, or at least in a separate court room with separate waiting accommodation. We think that ushers in courts dealing with family matters should be civilians and not police officers.

264. We understand that some adopters are reluctant to apply in the local magistrates' court because they fear that private information about them will be made known (albeit in confidence) to local people who know them or of them and before whom they must then appear. We suggest that this point could be met by relaxing, in adoption and guardianship cases, the rule which limits jurisdiction to a court acting for the area where the applicants or the child live; this relaxation should apply to relinquishment hearings as well as adoption hearings.

Expert evidence

265. In some adoption cases conflicting expert evidence is given on behalf of contending parties and it would be helpful if the court could obtain objective

and expert help. We understand that the High Court has power, of its own motion, to call expert witnesses, but that there is some doubt about whether lower courts have this power. In any event, the present law does not appear to make provision for the cost of such witnesses to be met. We consider that courts hearing adoption applications should have power to call expert witnesses, and that statutory provision should be made for the payment of costs, similar to the provisions for payment to witnesses called by the court in criminal cases. It should be borne in mind, however, that the calling of expert witnesses, where this involves repeated examinations of young children, should be kept to a minimum.

The hearing

266. The present law in England and Wales requires the attendance of the applicants at the hearing in the juvenile court and in the county court. The child also must be present unless there are special circumstances making this unnecessary. In the juvenile court proceedings are in camera and tend to be more formal; for example, where the hearing proceeds by formal question and answer from a witness box. The guardian presents his report to the court, sometimes on oath. County court applications are heard by a judge sitting alone in chambers. There is very little formality, the applicants not being required to present their application formally on oath where it is unopposed. The judge may have read the papers and the guardian's report beforehand. He may have questions to ask the applicants or the guardian. If the case is straightforward, hearings in the juvenile court and the county court are short. In High Court applications the applicants and the child are not required to attend in person, formal evidence being taken on affidavit.

267. The majority of applications in Scotland are granted without the applicants being present; and there has been no suggestion in the evidence that in Scotland applicants should be required to attend in all cases, or even more frequently than now. In England and Wales, however, most of the adoptive parents whose views were sought on some of the Committee's suggestions[2] thought that a hearing should continue to be necessary and that if given a choice they would have wanted to attend. It seems that in each country the present practice on this matter is accepted as satisfactory.

268. We have considered, in the light of our recommendations about relinquishment proceedings, whether the law in England and Wales should continue to require the presence of the applicants at the hearing of an adoption application. Where the mother has relinquished parental rights and an adoption application is subsequently made with the support of an agency, there seems no reason of principle or practice for regarding the presence of the applicants as automatically necessary. The fact that no reclaim of the child is possible will remove much of the anxiety which applicants now feel, and experience in Scotland suggests that if applicants are not led to expect a hearing they do not feel the lack of one. We recommend that the attendance of the applicants in such cases should be at the discretion of the court, although it should be open to them to attend if they wish. The absence of the applicants should not, however, affect the accountability of the agency to the court. If the agency wished to supplement orally its written report, or the court wished to question the agency, this could be arranged without the

presence of the applicants being required. In any case of doubt the court could be expected to hold a hearing with the applicants present and certainly before refusing an application.

269. We have received some evidence of dissatisfaction with present court procedures in unopposed cases, mainly because the hearing seems an anti-climax after months of waiting. When the applicants attend in cases where there is no dispute or disagreement, we think there should be sufficient solemnity, combined with an atmosphere of friendliness, to create a memorable occasion. The hearing should never be perfunctory and it should be clear to all that time and thought have been devoted to the application, with genuine concern for the welfare of the child. These aims can only in part be achieved by statutory provisions and rules of court. Much inevitably depends on the judge, or chairman of the bench who is responsible for the conduct of the hearing. It is important that judges and magistrates should be conscious of the importance of this aspect of adoption hearings.

270. The law requires adoption cases to be dealt with in private. We are sure that this is right and we recommend that this should also apply to guardianship applications.

Legal aid

271. Under the existing law, legal aid is already available in adoption cases where a parent or guardian wishes to contest an application to dispense with his consent to the adoption of his child; we think that the principle behind this provision is right. We recommend that the civil legal aid scheme in England and Wales should be extended so as to enable legal aid to be granted to any party to adoption proceedings where there is a dispute as to whether the court should grant the application (e.g. where the local authority oppose an application relating to a child in their care) and for the purpose of any appeal against the court's decision. (In Scotland legal aid is already available in these circumstances.) Legal aid is already available in guardianship proceedings and we recommend that it should be available in the extended guardianship proceedings we have recommended in Chapter 6. We deal in paragraph 255 with legal representation of the guardian ad litem.

272. We refer below to the importance of avoiding delay in the hearing of disputed adoption applications. Among the possible cause of delay is the time taken to consider an application for a legal aid certificate. We support the suggestion of Mr Justice Latey* that Legal Aid Committees should consider more readily the granting of emergency certificates, and that the legal advisers to the parties should help the Committees by drawing their attention to the urgency of adoption proceedings.

Delay

273. Where there is a dispute as to who shall care for a child, the persons who have the custody of the child, or their legal advisers, may not be anxious to hasten the hearing, feeling that the longer the child remains with them, the more unlikely is it that the court will disturb the situation. Since our

---

* *Re W*, Times Law Report, 27 January 1972.

appointment we have noted a number of reported cases in which the decision of the court was made more difficult by the time which had elapsed since the proceedings were started. In *O'Connor v A and B*, in which 2½ years elapsed between the child being placed for adoption and the final determination of the case by the House of Lords, Lord Simon of Glaisdale suggested that the problem of inevitable changes in circumstances pending an appeal might well claim our attention.*

274. We think that the only answer to this problem is expedition, at all levels, in hearing adoption cases. With regard to cases taken on appeal (e.g. to the Court of Appeal, or the House of Lords), we suggest for consideration a system under which applications could be made to the court whose decision is being appealed against, which will be aware of the circumstances of the case, for a certificate that the case is one of urgency. This certificate could then be attached to an application to the appellate court for the hearing of the appeal to be expedited. Consideration might also be given to the possibility of including in the rules of appellate courts provisions designed to ensure that adoption appeals are heard with a minimum of delay.

Recommendations

275. We make the following *recommendations* which need not await the outcome of the Law Commission's consideration of family courts.

> Adoption proceedings in magistrates' courts should be transferred from the juvenile court to the domestic court and arrangements should be made for the selection of suitable magistrates to sit in that court.
>
> (Recommendation 64)
>
> The rules which limit applications to courts in the applicants' or child's home area should be relaxed.
>
> (Recommendation 65)
>
> There should be power for the courts to summon expert witnesses if they consider this desirable, and the cost should be met from public funds.
>
> (Recommendation 66)
>
> Courts should have discretion whether to require the applicants for an adoption order to attend a hearing.
>
> (Recommendation 67)
>
> Legal aid should be available to all the parties at all stages in adoption proceedings where there is a dispute. Legal Aid Committees should consider more readily the granting of emergency certificates in adoption proceedings.
>
> (Recommendation 68)
>
> Courts at all levels should be aware of the need to avoid delay in hearing adoption cases. In the case of an appeal it should be possible to apply to the court whose decision is being appealed against for a certificate that the case is one of urgency.
>
> (Recommendation 69)

Family courts

276. We now turn to proposals for family courts in so far as they would

---

* [1971] 1 WLR 1227.

affect adoption and guardianship proceedings. This question is now being examined by the Law Commission and we make no recommendations on it. We regard this part of our report as a contribution to the work of the Law Commission, to whom we are making available the evidence we received.

277. The courts with adoption and guardianship jurisdiction deal also with other civil cases which concern family and personal problems and questions of personal status, and, in many cases, involve children. The Family Division of the High Court deals with defended divorces. Divorce county courts deal with undefended divorces. Magistrates' courts have jurisdiction to deal with matrimonial matters falling short of divorce, and also deal with affiliation.

278. These courts (the High Court, divorce county courts and magistrates' courts) are quite distinct from each other in the sense that each has its own separately defined jurisdiction and its own separate administrative arrangements. They are also distinct in that different kinds of persons serve in each court. Any unification of these arrangements, for example, by the establishment of a family court, must involve bringing together into a single jurisdiction the existing separate family jurisdictions, and establishing unified administrative arrangements in place of the existing separate ones. It would not necessarily follow, however, that the composition of the court should be the same in every case. It would be perfectly possible to have a family court with a unified jurisdiction and administration, but with a composition which varied according to the nature or difficulty of the case.

279. The object of any changes should be to improve the administration of justice and the standard of service to those who have recourse to the courts, not to produce changes which make the system appear tidier and more rational. Speed and accessibility are of particular importance. Many situations involving court proceedings are of a kind that ought to be resolved as soon as possible; this is certainly true of family matters, including adoptions and guardianship. We have referred in paragraphs 273 and 274 to the importance of avoiding delay. We think it is important that family courts should have a system of administrative support, perhaps on the lines recently introduced in the Crown Courts, and that among the administrator's responsibilities should be that of ensuring that there is no delay in hearing disputed cases.

Composition of a family court

280. The existing three tier system makes use of the resources of three courts. Any change which reduced the resources available for hearing family cases would cause considerable practical problems. Given a unified jurisdiction and administration, with arrangements for the allocation of cases to a court with the appropriate composition, we see attraction in the idea of a family court which would make use of the respective talents and experience of High Court Judges, circuit judges and lay magistrates.

281. In England and Wales the two main traditions in civil cases are a legally qualified person sitting alone (High Court Judge, circuit judge sitting in county courts, stipendiary magistrate); and a court consisting normally of three lay magistrates, including at least one of either sex, advised on matters

78

of law by their clerk. Both these traditions seem to be generally accepted; and if the work of dealing with family cases is to continue to be shared between judges and lay magistrates, we see no reason why cases of appropriate kinds should not continue to be heard by a court consisting of lay magistrates, receiving advice on the law from their clerk. Nor do we see any reason why a judge alone should not continue to decide cases. In the evidence about family courts the suggestion has been made that some kinds of family situation would benefit by being heard by a court consisting of, say, a legally qualified chairman and two lay magistrates. We see merit in this suggestion for cases involving complex legal issues which also require consideration of social factors. In such a court each member would be able to bring to bear his or her own experience and understanding, there would be opportunity for discussion before the final decision was taken, it could be ensured that both sexes were represented, and the expertise of the family court chairman would assist in securing the clear and orderly presentation of the evidence, consideration of the issues and formulation of the judgment. The administrative machinery which we envisage as part of the family court structure would be used to allocate cases to the different kinds of court.

282. Under the present system, judges and magistrates who hear family cases are selected because they have qualifications and experience fitting them for the whole range of duties of a judge or magistrate rather than for this particular aspect, although they gain considerable experience of it in the course of their work. The establishment of a family court would, we suggest, involve a degree of specialisation in adjudication on family matters that should be reflected in the arrangements for selection and training. We envisage that the qualifications and experience of family court judges would include a wider knowledge of social services and social administration as well as traditional legal training, and we agree with the view of the Ormrod Committee[22] that there is as much need for conferences for judges exercising family jurisdiction as for "sentencing conferences" for criminal judges. All newly appointed magistrates now receive training, but it is only for work in the juvenile court that a special panel of magistrates is selected and that additional specialised training is provided. Similar arrangements for specialised training might be made for magistrates selected to sit in family courts.

SCOTLAND

283. In Scotland at the present time two courts have jurisdiction of first instance in adoption cases—the Court of Session (Inner House) and the sheriff court. Adoption applications to the Court of Session are rare, only two being dealt with in 1971 as compared with 1,925 applications to the sheriff court. In practical terms, therefore, adoption jurisdiction is almost totally confined to the sheriff court.

284. The Court of Session has exclusive jurisdiction in actions of divorce and other actions (e.g. nullity of marriage) which involve the personal status of the individual. The Court of Session also has a concurrent jurisdiction with the sheriff court in all other matters connected with the family and children, whether legitimate or illegitimate; but in practice, with the important exception

of divorce, it is the sheriff courts which exercise this jurisdiction, disposing (in 1970) of 573 actions relating to separation, aliment etc. and 302 actions of affiliation and aliment, as well as dealing with questions affecting the custody of children.

285. The Scottish system at present therefore comes closer to a unified court system than does the English system; and the only change in jurisdiction which we proposed in our working paper was that those adoption cases which go to the Court of Session at first instance should be transferred from the Inner to the Outer House. The considerations governing this proposal were (a) that since divorce, custody and separation actions are dealt with by the Outer House there appeared to be no reason why adoption cases should be reserved to the Inner House; and (b) that since appeal jurisdiction in adoption matters lies with the Inner House it seemed inappropriate that jurisdiction of first instance—no matter how infrequent the cases—should also lie there.

286. The proposition in our working paper that adoption jurisdiction should remain with the sheriff court and the Court of Session, but with transfer from the Inner to the Outer House of the latter, met with general approval in both legal and social work circles; and we therefore recommend accordingly. The effects would be that in the future, as now, virtually all adoption cases would go to the sheriff court, and that cases arising from the wider facility to apply for guardianship which we recommend elsewhere in our report would go there also.

287. In our working paper we suggested that there might be cases in which a sheriff, while not considering there to be a need for a curator ad litem to make specific enquiries on behalf of the court, might nevertheless wish to have the help of a professional expert in weighing up the evidence. We suggested therefore that the sheriff should be empowered, at his own discretion, to sit with expert assessors; and that an approved list of assessors (who might be qualified in medicine or social work) should be drawn up.

288. Legal opinion in Scotland was against these suggestions, which were regarded as constituting a potential diminution of the role of the courts. The bodies representing social work practitioners were on the other hand generally in favour of the proposals. Some of the evidence presented to us suggested that medical assessors would have to be particularly qualified in the area of adoption medical practice which the court was examining; and there were those who made the point that the range of expertise from which assessors were drawn might have to be extended to include, for example, psychologists.

289. There are statutory precedents, some of long standing, for enabling courts in Scotland to appoint expert assessors (Nautical Assessors (Scotland) Act 1894; Coal-Mining (Subsidence) Act 1957). We envisage that the power would be used sparingly in relation to adoption proceedings, usually in opposed cases; but we consider nevertheless that it would be useful to courts to have the power. We consider that the power should be exercised by the court on its own motion, on the joint motion of the parties, or, if the court agrees, on the motion of one party.

290. Although no evidence was presented specifically on the question of an "approved list" of assessors, we have reviewed this concept in the light of the comments that the range of expertise might have to be extended beyond the fields of medicine and social work. We accept the validity of these comments; and it now seems to us that, given the diversity of matters which may be at issue in adoption proceedings, it may not be practicable to envisage in advance of those proceedings the total range of special knowledge that might be needed. There is the allied consideration that, with the speed of the advance of knowledge and increasing specialisation, a list approved at any given time could go rapidly out of date. We therefore consider it preferable that a court requiring an expert assessor in a particular field and in relation to a particular case should seek at that time the advice of the professional organisation concerned with the speciality in question. Depending on the nature of the organisation's own internal arrangements, this could be done by an approach at either national or local level.

291. At present the majority of adoption applications in Scotland are granted without a hearing, this being a substantial difference between Scottish and English procedure. We considered in our working paper whether to suggest a change in the Scottish practice, but decided against this; we suggested therefore that it should continue to be within the sheriff's discretion to decide whether there should be a hearing for an adoption application, and that this discretion should be extended to guardianship applications by relatives or foster parents.

292. Our suggestions met with a considerable measure of approval, the only reservations, expressed by one organisation, being that they should not apply to guardianship applications by foster parents. We do not see sufficient ground for excluding this particular category of applications from the sheriff's discretion, and we consider that our original proposition should stand in this respect. There should, of course, be adequate contact between the sheriff and the adoption agency or curator, regardless of whether there is a hearing or not.

293. We referred in paragraphs 273 and 274, in relation to England and Wales, to the importance of avoiding delay in the hearing of adoption cases. This is equally important in Scotland and our recommendation No 69 should apply to Scotland.

Recommendations

294. *We recommend* that:—

> Adoption jurisdiction at first instance in Scotland should remain with the sheriff court and the Court of Session, but should be transferred from the Inner to the Outer House of the latter court.
>
> (Recommendation 70)
>
> The court should be empowered, either on its own motion, or on the joint motion of the parties, or—with its agreement—on the motion of one party, to appoint expert assessors to assist in the weighing up of evidence. Where expert assessors are required they should be chosen in consultation

with the professional organisations concerned, and the cost should be met from public funds.

(Recommendation 71)

It should be within the discretion of the court to decide whether there should be a hearing for adoption applications, or applications for guardianship by relatives or foster parents. Whether there is a hearing or not, there should be adequate contact between the sheriff and the adoption agency or curator.

(Recommendation 72)

Recommendation No 69 (avoidance of delay) should apply to Scotland.

(Recommendation 73)

CHAPTER 11

MISCELLANEOUS

The link between natural parents and adopted child

295. The issues of whether, in an adoption application, the identity of the natural parents should be concealed from the adopters, and whether and to what extent an adopted child should have a right to know his origin and background are interlinked. Adoptive applicants who wish their identity to be kept confidential may apply to the court under a serial number. But the names of the natural parents are known to the adoptive applicants because they appear on the consent form, on the child's birth certificate and on the application form for an adoption order.

Anonymity for the adopters

296. We fully accept the need for adoptive parents to be open and frank with the child about the fact that he is adopted, and that an adopted child should have a right—indeed he has a need—to know about his natural parents and his background (see paragraph 28). At the same time, anonymity serves as a protection for both parties—for the adoptive parents against interference from the natural parents or the fear of this, and for the natural parents against any interference from the adopters or any temptation to watch the child's progress or in other ways to feel the links still in existence. There was no evidence to suggest that adopters should not still be able to conceal their names from the natural parents and we regard it as a desirable protection.

Anonymity for the natural parents

297. In our working paper we suggested that the natural parents should also be able to choose to be referred to by serial number in adoption proceedings to preserve their anonymity. Although the evidence was numerically in favour of this proposition, there were thoughtful contributions to the contrary. There was concern lest the child's natural identity should be obscured in this way, with the result that his original surname might be withheld from him for ever. Other evidence pointed out the inconsistency of extending the secrecy of adoption while advocating a more open approach to the subject, and referred to the safeguard against inter-marriage of siblings afforded by the knowledge of the original surnames.

298. Natural parents in general may not need the same protection of anonymity as adoptive parents, but there can be cases where the parents strongly wish to retain anonymity because they are well known or belong to closely knit communities in which the child might be placed for adoption. On balance we think that, in cases where children are relinquished for adoption, the parents should have the right, if they wish, to be completely anonymous as far as the adopters are concerned until the adoption process is completed. We think that it may be possible to provide for this without introducing a formal serial number procedure because parental rights will have been relinquished to an

agency and at the adoption hearing the natural parents will not be parties to the proceedings. However, we take the view that the child's original name should not be concealed from the adopters once the adoption process has been completed, and that it should appear in full on the form of adoption order which is given to the adopters. We recognise that in the case of an unusual surname this may lessen the degree of anonymity afforded to the natural parents, but we consider that in the interests of the child this must be accepted. In the case of adoptions by relatives or foster parents, or any other case where parental rights are not relinquished in advance of the adoption hearing, we do not think it will be possible to provide for anonymity in this way.

Information for the child

299. The responsibility for telling a child that he is adopted and later giving him information about his natural parents rests primarily upon the adopters. Many adopters do not find it easy to discharge this responsibility and may require help to do so. We consider that when an agency has arranged an adoption, it has an obligation to offer not only social work help and advice up to the time of the hearing, but also a counselling service thereafter. Background information about the child should normally be given in writing to the adopters by the agency at the time of adoption, and we recommend that the name of the adoption agency should appear on the order so that the adopted person may himself later be in a position to approach the agency for information that the adopters are unable or unwilling to provide. In our view it is generally right for most if not all of the available background information to be given to an adopted person who seeks it. It appears to us that such disclosure is already permitted by Regulation 7 of the Adoption Agencies Regulations. The adopted person's need for help of this sort may not arise until comparatively late in life, and we therefore recommend that agencies should be required to retain their records for 75 years and to transfer them to a successor agency or the local authority if they cease to be registered. The registering authority should keep an up-to-date list of the location of the records of all adoption agencies, including those no longer registered.

Access to birth records

300. In Scotland an adopted child has the right at the age of 17 to obtain a copy of the original entry relating to his birth; he has also the right upon application to the court which made the adoption order to see the court records of the adoption proceedings (known in Scotland as the process). In England and Wales an adopted person can obtain a copy of his original birth entry only under an order of the High Court, the Westminster County Court or the court by which the adoption order was made. We suggested in our working paper that there should be no change in the position in England and Wales, but we proposed to reconsider the position in Scotland in the light of research[7] being undertaken there. The results of this research have now been made available to us and we summarise it in the following paragraph.

301. The aim of the research was to test the hypothesis that the provision enabling a person adopted in Scotland to obtain a copy of his original birth certificate is of positive value to adopted persons. Over 40 adopted persons a year apply to the Registrar General in Scotland for information from their

original birth record. Dr Triseliotis interviewed 70 people* who applied and found that the provision was of some value to adopted people who had been deprived of important information about their biological and sociological background. It seems that where an adopted person has been told of his adoption at an early age and his relationship with his adopters is good he is less likely to seek access to his original birth record. Two-thirds of those in the sample who sought this information came to know about their adoption when they were eleven or more years old, half of them being 16 or over and one as old as 40. Only two-fifths of those who applied had been told of their adoption by their adoptive parents, the others finding out by discovering documents or letters or from chance remarks by people outside the family, mainly other children. For many of them the late disclosure of their adoption came as a shock, and they had difficulty in coming to terms with it. It was also noticeable that two out of every five who sought this information had lost one or both adoptive parents by death, separation or divorce before they reached the age of 16, and in one-third of all the applications it was the death of an adoptive parent that triggered off the search for information about the natural parents. Two-thirds of those who sought this information had the immediate reaction that it was helpful or of some help to them, while one-third felt very upset by the information they had obtained. Some were unhappy to discover that they were illegitimate, while the few who were legitimate were equally sad to think that their parents, although married, had "given them away". When seen four months later, however, nine out of ten had no regrets about having taken steps to find out this information.

302. The other evidence we received was divided. Although there was support for the view that access to birth records should be granted only by a court in England and Wales, there was strong opposition to the suggestion that the present right of children adopted in Scotland should be withdrawn. Some witnesses urged that the right of an adult adopted person to know the names of his natural parents was a basic human right. Others were concerned about the distress which might be caused as a result of widespread attempts by adopted children to seek out their original parents. The Scottish research showed that although 42 adopted persons, or 60 per cent of the sample, sought to trace their natural parents, only four succeeded in doing so, although seven others were able to contact blood relations. The Deputy Registrar General for Scotland said that he could not recall any complaint made by natural relatives who had been traced through the Registrar General's records. The fear of being traced may therefore have been unduly magnified, particularly as all the indications are that the climate of opinion is changing and mothers are becoming less concerned to conceal the fact that they have had an illegitimate child. Research[2] into the views of a sample of adoptive parents revealed that 63 per cent considered that their adoptive children should be allowed free access to their original records.

303. The weight of the evidence as a whole was in favour of freer access to background information, and this accords with our wish to encourage greater openness about adoption. We take the view that on reaching the age of

---

* Although this was a fairly small sample, the number interviewed was more than the average number of adopted persons seeking their original birth records in any one year.

majority an adopted person should not be denied access to his original birth records. We therefore recommend that all adopted adults in England and Wales, whenever adopted, should in future be permitted to obtain a copy of their original birth entry, and that in Scotland the age at which access to original birth records is permitted should similarly be 18, instead of 17 as at present.

304. The evidence suggests that those who are sufficiently concerned to seek this information often need more help than mere knowledge of the facts recorded in the register can be expected to afford them. We were impressed by the sympathetic way in which enquiries in Scotland are handled by the Registrar General's staff, but we think that many adopted persons who seek their original birth record need more help in dealing with problems of identity and more information of a kind that will be helpful to them. We therefore suggest that all adopted adults who apply either in person or in writing to either of the two General Register Offices for access to their original birth records should be advised, at the time that their original birth certificate is handed or sent to them, that if they would like further help or information the agency which arranged the adoption or the social services department (or social work department in Scotland) of the local authority in whose area they live would be willing to discuss the matter with them. Where this is done by post, a personal letter rather than a leaflet would seem appropriate.

305. While we consider that an adult adopted person should have an automatic right to a copy of his original birth certificate, we do not consider it desirable that he should automatically be granted access to the court records of the adoption proceedings as is at present the case in Scotland. We think that, in both countries, it should be open to an adopted person to apply to the court for the disclosure of information from the court records of the adoption proceedings, but the court should have discretion to grant or refuse the application. In future the agency will always be named on the adoption order (see paragraph 299) and we think that, if the applicant is not in possession of an adoption order giving this information, the court should be prepared to disclose to him the name of the agency, if any, so that he can seek further help from them if he wishes.

Recommendations

306. *We recommend* that:—

Natural parents who relinquish their children for adoption should be able to be anonymous so far as the adopters are concerned.

(Recommendation 74)

The adoption agency or, where there is no agency, the local authority, should be named on the adoption order.

(Recommendation 75)

Arrangements should be made for the preservation of adoption records for 75 years.

(Recommendation 76)

An adopted person aged 18 years or over should be entitled to a copy of his original birth certificate.

(Recommendation 77)

Courts should have discretion to grant or refuse an application from an adopted person for the disclosure of information from the court records of the adoption proceedings.

(Recommendation 78)

The position when the court does not make a final order:
Where the order is refused

307. At present where the court refuses to make an adoption order in respect of a child placed by an agency, or the application is withdrawn, the child must be returned to the agency concerned within seven days of notice of withdrawal or of refusal (section 35(3) of the 1958 Act). It was suggested to us that a court ought to be able to extend the period in which the child is to be handed over so as to allow for a gradual introduction of the child into a new home, particularly in the case of older children, and to provide more time for applicants to consider an appeal where the application was refused because the mother had withdrawn her consent. We recommend that the court should have discretion to extend the hand-over period up to a maximum of six weeks.

308. In a non-agency placement the child remains in the applicants' home even though the court has refused to make an adoption order, unless the natural parent chooses to reclaim her child. We suggested in our working paper that in order to protect the child in these cases the court should be able to make an alternative order such as a supervision order or an order committing the child to the care of the local authority. There was general agreement with this suggestion.

Interim orders

309. Section 8 of the 1958 Act gives the court power to postpone the determination of an adoption application and to make an interim order giving the custody of the child to the applicants for a probationary period not exceeding two years. Comparatively few interim orders* are made each year and what evidence there is indicates that many relate to applications by step-parents and grandparents about which the court is not wholly satisfied. Unless the situation deteriorates badly, a court is unlikely to refuse a full adoption order after the child has become established in the home, and in fact it is rare for an interim order not to be followed by a full order. We suggested in our working paper that, where a court is in doubt about the suitability of a placement, or where further information is required, an adjournment is more appropriate than an interim order.

310. The evidence was predominantly in agreement with our suggestion, but it was put to us that the court should remain able to follow either course. We expect that our earlier recommendations on improving agency standards, the banning of independent placements with non-relatives and the alternative of guardianship for step-parents and relatives, will greatly reduce the need for interim orders and adjournments. We have considered whether in these circumstances the retention of the interim order would be justified. An

---

* 32 interim orders were made by juvenile courts in England and Wales in 1969; figures for other courts are not available.

interim order has certain advantages over an adjournment. One is that the parent may not apply to the court for permission to remove the child during the currency of the order. A second is that the adoption agency or the guardian ad litem remains in contact with the adoptive home during the period of the order and can help with any difficulty. We accept therefore that the power to make interim orders should be retained, although in future they will rarely be necessary. We consider that an appeal should be possible against the decision of any court to make an interim order, since it is in the child's interest that any objections to the adoption should be considered at that stage and not deferred for anything up to two years until an adoption order is made or otherwise. (A right of appeal against an interim order made by a county court judge already exists. The right of appeal in Scotland is not clear, no appeal having been attempted there, but we consider that such right should be made explicit in the law.)

Recommendations

311. We accordingly *recommend* that:—

Where a court refuses an application for an adoption order it should have discretion to extend the period for the return of the child to the agency up to a maximum of six weeks.

(Recommendation 79)

Where a court refuses an application for an adoption order in non-agency cases, it should have power to make an alternative order, i.e. a supervision order or an order committing the child to the care of the local authority.

(Recommendation 80)

There should be a right of appeal against an interim order made by any court.

(Recommendation 81)

Provisional adoption orders

312. The Adoption of Children (Regulation) Act 1939 (following the report of the Horsbrugh Committee[12]) prohibited the transfer of a child to a foreigner who was not the guardian or a relative of the child; and prohibited the transfer of a child to a British subject, resident abroad, who was not his guardian or a relative, except with a licence. The licensing jurisdiction rested with the Chief Metropolitan Magistrate and the magistrates at Bow Street Court. The legislation did not require the appointment of a guardian ad litem or the presence of the prospective "adopters" at the hearing. There were two important disadvantages in the licensing system. A licence gave no security to the adopters, the parents, or the child, since the rights and obligations of parents were not transferred (although their consent was necessary). Moreover, a child could be sent abroad without the applicants ever having seen him.

313. The Hurst Committee[8] re-considered this question. They considered that domicile should be the basis of eligibility to apply for an adoption order. The recommendations they made with regard to British people domiciled here but resident abroad are now the basis of section 12 of the 1958 Act. With regard to persons not domiciled here, they saw no reason why licences

should be granted only to British subjects. They considered that a probationary period, with the child living with the applicants, was necessary before a licence was granted. They thought that the procedure for applying for a licence should be similar to the procedure for applying for an adoption order, including supervision by the local authority and enquiries by a guardian ad litem. Parental consent would be required and would include consent to the vesting of parental rights in the applicants. Licences would continue to be granted by the Chief Metropolitan Magistrate or the Bow Street Magistrates' Court. The 1958 Act departed from these recommendations to the extent that it substituted for the Bow Street licence a provisional adoption order obtainable from any court (other than a juvenile court) empowered to make adoption orders. A provisional adoption order, like the former Bow Street licence, can be effective only in this country.

314. Section 52 of the 1958 Act makes it unlawful for anyone to take or send a British child out of the country with a view to adoption by any person other than a parent, guardian or relative unless a provisional adoption order has first been obtained. Section 53 of the 1958 Act provides that where a person not domiciled in this country (and therefore unable to obtain a full order here) wishes to remove a child for adoption in the country in which he is domiciled, a court may make a provisional adoption order giving him interim custody and authority to take the child out of the country. Applications for provisional adoption orders must be made to the High Court or a county court or in Scotland to the Court of Session or sheriff court. The applicant must satisfy the requirements for a full adoption order in this country (except domicile) and must have had care or possession of the child for at least six consecutive months immediately before the date of the order instead of the usual three months.

315. The number of provisional adoption orders is comparatively small, the figures in each year since 1965 having been fewer than 200 in England and Wales and fewer than 30 in Scotland. (In 1970, in 97 of the total of 173 provisional adoptions one of the applicants was a parent of the child and could have taken the child abroad for adoption without a provisional adoption order.)

316. We referred in our working paper to concern which had been expressed about these orders because there was no means of ensuring that the child would be adopted in the country to which he was taken. This concern was repeated in the evidence we received. It was pointed out that the adopters' marriage could break down and, unless an adoption order had been made in the country concerned, the child's legal status would be uncertain.

317. Although the court is required to be satisfied that the applicant for a provisional adoption order intends to adopt the child under the law of, or within, the country in which he is domiciled, there is no way in which persons who have obtained a provisional adoption order can be made to do so after they have arrived in that country. The only alternative to the existing procedure would be a complete ban on taking children abroad for the purposes of adoption. Since this could easily be evaded it would mean the abrogation of any control. Moreover, there are children to whom a foreign couple, perhaps of

the same race, might offer a very suitable home in another country. A complete ban would prevent this, except where the law was evaded, when there would be no assessment of the situation by the courts and agencies. We consider, therefore, that the power to make provisional orders should remain.

318. Applicants are already required by section 53 of the 1958 Act to have care and possession for at least six months, under the supervision of the local authority concerned, before an order can be made. This prevents casual adoption by foreign visitors and tends to limit provisional adoption to people who are temporarily working in this country. Many provisional orders have been made on the application of American servicemen, sometimes following marriage to the child's mother and sometimes for the adoption of an unrelated child. We have recommended earlier that it should be an offence for a person other than a registered adoption agency to place a child, for the purpose of adoption, with non-relatives and we recommend that this should apply also to placements for the-purpose of a provisional adoption order. We consider that the agency concerned should, as part of its investigations, get in touch with an adoption agency in the applicants' country of domicile. The object would be to enquire about their background and to put the foreign agency in touch with the adopters with a view to the case being followed up and everything possible being done to see that a full adoption order was sought in the country concerned when the family returned there. The report of the British agency to the court should indicate the results of these enquiries.

319. A provisional adoption order authorises the applicant to take the child out of the country for the purpose of adoption and it also gives him custody of the child pending the adoption. This is not always understood in the country to which the child goes and the orders have been criticised for this reason. We have considered whether the name of the order should be changed, but we are doubtful whether this would help. We suggest that an explanation of the purpose and effect of a provisional adoption order should be incorporated in the order itself or set out in a note attached to it. We consider that the form of the order should be redrafted to make its effect clear, and should include a request to the overseas court making a final order that a copy of the order be sent to the Registrar General in this country. This would enable a check to be kept on the extent to which children who go abroad for adoption are in fact legally adopted.

320. Relatives, as defined in the Adoption Act 1958,* do not need a provisional adoption order to take a child abroad. There may be occasions, however, where a more distant relative domiciled abroad wishes to adopt a child who is here, perhaps when a child has been orphaned. It may not be possible for the relative to fulfil the six month's care and possession requirement and in these circumstances a simpler procedure may be appropriate, possibly on the lines of the power of the Secretary of State to authorise the emigration of children in care (section 17 of the Children Act 1948 and section 23 of the Social Work (Scotland) Act 1968).

---

* "Relative" for the purposes of the 1958 Act means a grandparent, brother, sister, uncle or aunt, whether of full-blood or by affinity, and includes a natural father.

Recommendation

321. We accordingly *recommend* that:—

> The power to make provisional adoption orders should remain, but there should be improvements in practice and the form of such orders should be redrafted.

(Recommendation 82)

Children from overseas

322. Children coming for adoption from overseas countries are subject to the same controls as other persons coming for permanent residence here. Where a visa or entry permit has to be obtained in advance there is an opportunity to make enquiries about the suitability of the proposed adopters. In the case of a child from a foreign country with which the United Kingdom has a visa abolition agreement, nothing may be known of the proposed adoption until the child arrives at a United Kingdom port. If the child is unescorted, or escorted by someone who has agreed to care for the child for the duration of the journey only, the child may have to be admitted without enquiries being made about the proposed adopters. The position may be further complicated by an adoption order having been obtained by proxy in the child's country of origin. The placement, which may have been arranged entirely by correspondence, may break down, or an adoption order may be refused, or not sought, leaving the child in the United Kingdom with no legal parent or guardian.

323. We have already recommended that only a registered adoption agency should be permitted to place a child with non-relatives, and we consider that the arguments in support of that recommendation apply with even greater force to the placement of children from overseas. These placements come within the category of independent placements, in that they take place without the intervention of an adoption agency registered in this country. Some may be arranged by private individuals, here or overseas, others by foreign adoption agencies, others direct between a children's home or organisation in the overseas country with a couple living here. The placements have all the potential disadvantages of independent placements which we have described in paragraph 84 above. In addition, the children are particularly vulnerable for a number of reasons. For instance, the child is often beyond infancy, and at an age when transfer from one environment to another may be particularly hazardous. There may be health problems, with difficulty in getting a full medical history. Of the greatest concern is the usual absence of information about the natural parents and the child's natural family circumstances. When the child has been in public care his legal position is often in doubt, so that the grant of an adoption order has to be delayed while enquiries are made in the country of origin and in the end the court may still be faced with a request to dispense with parental consent to adoption with no possibility of knowing whether the child was really abandoned. Finally, the British Adoption Project experiment has shown that the nature of a cross-cultural adoption is such that adoptive parents can and do benefit by special help and preparation to understand the implications.

324. We suggested in our working paper that it might be made an offence to receive a child for adoption except through an adoption agency registered in

91

this country. There was a large measure of agreement in the evidence with the need to provide safeguards for children from overseas and with the suggestions we made. We have accordingly recommended in Chapter 4 that, besides its being an offence for a person other than an adoption agency registered in this country to place a child for adoption, it should also be an offence to receive a child for adoption otherwise than through an adoption agency registered in this country. It would not be possible to impose sanctions on agencies or individuals in foreign countries, but the second recommendation, in particular, would restrict the reception of children from overseas. An appropriate way of handling these cases would be through the intermediary of an agency such as International Social Service of Great Britain, which, we understand, would be prepared to deal with enquiries from persons who wish to adopt children from overseas, and to accept or assist in the reception of a limited number of such children working in co-operation with appropriate overseas agencies.

325. We make no recommendation on this point because Recommendations 13 and 14 will prevent the placement and reception of children from overseas except through an adoption agency registered in this country.

Interpretation of wills and other instruments

326. The present law provides that for the purposes of inheritance (in Scotland, succession) and of the interpretation of dispositions made after an adoption order, an adopted person shall be treated as if he is a child born to the adopter in lawful wedlock and not the child of any other person. This means that an adopted child has the same rights on an intestacy occurring after the adoption order as a child born to the adopter in wedlock. In England and Wales an adopted person does not, however, benefit under a general gift to, say, grandchildren of the testator, where the disposition was made before the date of the adoption order unless it can be construed to include adopted children as such. (A will for this purpose is treated as having been made on the date of the death of the testator and not on the date the will was actually made.) For example, a man might leave part of his estate on trust to his wife for life, to be divided on her death among his grand-children. A natural grandchild born after his death would benefit under this will, but a grandchild by adoption would not.

327. If adoption means the complete severance of the legal relationship between the child and his natural parents and the establishment of a new and irrevocable relationship, designed to make the child a full member of another family, it follows that that child should have exactly the same rights under wills and other instruments as a natural child of the adoptive family.* We proposed that this should be the case and none of the evidence dissented from our proposition. It was pointed out to us that the passing of the Family Law Reform Act 1969 had placed illegitimate children in England and Wales in a better position than adopted children by providing, in section 15, that an illegitimate child may take under any disposition made after the Act came into force whether he was born before or after the disposition.

* Subject to the transitional provisions contained in section 5 of the Law Reform (Miscellaneous Provisions) (Scotland) Act 1966, this had already been achieved for Scotland by section 23 of the Succession (Scotland) Act 1964.

Recommendation

328. *We recommend* that:—

An adopted child should have exactly the same rights under wills and other instruments as a natural child of the adoptive family.

(Recommendation 83)

Marriage

329. Under the law as it stands an adopter and the person whom he has been authorised to adopt are not allowed to marry, but a person may marry his relations by adoption, including his brother or sister, if they are not otherwise within the prohibited degrees of marriage.

330. In our working paper we referred to the feelings against marriage between natural and adoptive children and we said that, on balance, we thought that it should be prohibited for adopted children to marry anyone whom they would have been debarred from marrying if they had been born, rather than adopted into that family, save that it should be open to them to apply to a court for special permission to marry.

331. Numerically the evidence supported the proposition, but there were strong opinions in favour of leaving the law as it is. It was pointed out that for biological reasons an adopted child remains subject to marriage prohibitions in relation to his natural family, and an extension of prohibitions on marriage to the adoptive relations would make him subject to two sets of prohibitions. Both the Law Commission for England and Wales and the Kilbrandon Committee on the Law of Marriage in Scotland have considered this issue. The Kilbrandon Committee advocated the extension of the law so as to prohibit marriage between an adopted person and his or her sister and brother and niece and nephew in the adoptive relationship, but would have allowed an adopted child to marry his or her aunt or uncle by adoption. The English Law Commission would prefer to leave the law unchanged. They doubt whether the compromise solution of leaving the court to decide is satisfactory, because it presupposes that in some circumstances it is a good thing for adopted children to marry within the adoptive family and in others it is not, and that there are justiciable criteria for distinguishing between these circumstances; they questioned whether these assumptions were well founded. They also pointed out that a couple who had reached the stage of applying to a court might well decide to live together, whatever the result of their application.

332. Marriages between adopted persons and their close relatives by adoption have been permitted since adoption law was introduced more than 40 years ago and were permitted before that when all adoptions were *de facto*. A complete ban, whether limited to siblings by adoption or with a wider application, might cause distress to a small number of people. Recent research[2] has shown that only 27 per cent of adoptive parents consulted would favour a complete ban on marriage between siblings by adoption. We accept the Law Commission's argument that it is difficult to see on what grounds a court, given discretion, could identify cases in which it would be proper to refuse permission to marry to two adults, when there were no biological objections.

Recommendation

333. We accordingly *recommend* that:—

The present prohibitions on marriage should not be extended.

(Recommendation 84)

Committees

334. The Adoption Agencies Regulations 1959 and the corresponding Scottish regulations place duties on the society's "case committees". Regulation 5 requires certain of the enquiries in regard to prospective adopters to be made "by or on behalf of the society's case committee", and requires the case committee to approve the placement of a child. Under Regulation 6 the case committee decides how often the child has to be visited by the agency in the adoptive home after placement and receives reports as to his welfare. Regulation 10 specifies the composition of the case committee of a registered adoption society. Regulations 5 and 6 apply to a local authority making or participating in arrangements for the adoption of children, "except that any reference therein to the case committee of a registered adoption society shall be construed as a reference to the local authority" (Regulation 9).

335. We described in our working paper the variations in the use of committees by agencies and the confusion as to their purpose. This was substantiated by a survey carried out by the Association of British Adoption Agencies.[23] The suggestions we made rested on certain principles: the importance of an established machinery for decision-making; the distinction between policy and case decisions; the need for case decisions to be group decisions; the distinction of role between the committee members and social work staff of the agency.

336. The evidence we received disclosed a variety of views and reflected the differences between local authorities and voluntary societies. There was general agreement with the suggestions we made, except that some witnesses saw no objection to suitable lay members taking part in casework practice, for instance, by interviewing prospective applicants.

337. The purpose of a case committee is to bring an objective and independent, as well as knowledgeable, viewpoint to bear on a decision. We consider that case decisions, whether in regard to the acceptance of adoptive applicants or the placement of the child, should always be made by a group, whether of professionals or of mixed professional and lay members. The social workers concerned with the case should be present and participate in the discussion.

338. We remain of the opinion that lay members should not be used as professional workers. The social work tasks of the agency should be carried out by the professional workers of the agency, identified with and accountable to the agency, some of whom may be members of a case committee under the arrangements described above. Lay committee members have a different role. They bring an outside, objective viewpoint, and are an important link with the community. This role is incompatible with that of a voluntary worker involved in casework.

94

339. In regard to an agency's policy committee, we think that this should consist predominantly of lay members, but should have professional advice. Although it should not take casework decisions we think it essential that this committee should keep in touch with developments in practice.

340. In Chapter 3 and in Appendix C we have recommended that the committee structure of an agency and the decision-making arrangements should be matters which the Secretary of State should consider when deciding whether to register a voluntary agency. In view of this, we do not think it necessary to prescribe in statutory regulations the composition and functions of committees.

Recommendations
341. *We recommend* that:—
All agencies should have an established machinery for making decisions.
(Recommendation 85)
Policy decisions will normally be taken by the controlling committee, which could include both lay members and professional workers. Case decisions should always be group decisions, either by a professional group or a mixed professional and lay group.
(Recommendation 86)
Casework should not be undertaken by committee members who are not professional social workers.
(Recommendation 87)

The medical aspects of adoption
342. The importance of the medical aspects of adoption, including mental health, should be adequately recognised both in the law and in practice. First, it is essential that a child should be placed with people who are likely, as far as can reasonably be ascertained, to have a good expectation of life and to enjoy satisfactory physical health and emotional stability, at least until the child has reached the age of independence. Secondly, the adoptive parents should be aware of any medical problems in the child or his family background so that they can make a decision to accept the child in the full knowledge of the facts and be aware of any special needs he may have in the future.

343. In the medical aspects of adoption, as in other aspects, law and practice are inextricably interwoven. We think that the medical arrangements of adoption agencies should be covered by the registration procedures, and standards assessed by the registering authority. The medical requirements for the purpose of the court application should be defined by the law, which should also prescribe the broad framework for the medical arrangements within which agencies should operate. Our suggestions about agency practice are what we consider should be the aim.

Medical requirements relating to the child
344. In the past some children have not been accepted for adoption because of trivial abnormalities or because the family health history has included mental or physical disease. With the increasing knowledge and contribution of paediatrics and medical genetics to these problems, a much clearer estimate of the degree of a child's risk of developing such conditions can be obtained,

and many such children could be accepted and placed for adoption. We consider that it should become standard practice for every agency to have a paediatric adviser who will be available to help with medical problems arising in the child or on account of his natural family. In this way more children will be offered for adoption who, in the past, have not been placed because of supposed health problems.

345. The present law requires an agency to obtain a medical report, on a prescribed form, before the child is placed.* In England and Wales the court rules require the adoption application to be accompanied by a statement of the child's health unless the applicant is a parent or relative or the child is over compulsory school age.† A report to the court is not required by law in Scotland, although the report of the pre-placement examination may be made available to the court if required. The form prescribed for this purpose in England and Wales is similar to that prescribed by the Adoption Agencies Regulations. The object of prescribing the same form was to enable the report of the pre-placement examination to be used for the purpose of the application to the court, so that the same examination could serve both purposes, although, in practice, the time limits make this impracticable in many cases.

346. In agency adoptions, developments in practice have moved ahead of the legal requirements. It has been found that a detailed and comprehensive medical examination is essential to good practice before the child is placed; some agencies already arrange such an examination and forms specially prepared by the Medical Group of the Association of British Adoption Agencies are increasingly being used. The form prescribed in the Rules is used, in England and Wales, for the medical report to the court. This form needs revision as it omits the family health history and requires little comment on the child's development.

347. The evidence supported the view expressed in our working paper that the law should continue to require a pre-placement examination and that, before the hearing of the adoption application, there should be a further examination, the result of which should be reported to the court. The two examinations have a different purpose. The purpose of the first is to obtain a clear picture of the present condition of the child and his probable future development in the light of his age, his own and his family history, so that suitable adopters can be sought who can be given full information about him and who then feel able to accept and deal with any health problems there may be. The purpose of the second examination is two-fold: first, to provide the adopters with an up-to-date assessment of the child's health and development; second, to provide recent information to assist the court in its independent assessment as to whether an adoption order should be made. In the very young child certain medical conditions may not be apparent at the age of a few days or weeks when the pre-placement examination may be made. Where the placement of an older child is concerned, he will usually be observed for several months in his adoptive home before the formalities are completed, and during this time further health and developmental studies can be made.

* Adoption Agencies Regulations 1959, regulation 5. The Adoption Agencies (Scotland) Regulations 1959, regulation 5.
† Adoption (Juvenile Court) Rules 1959, First Schedule, forms 1 and 3.

We recommend that the medical report for the court should relate to a recent examination, which, especially in the case of an infant, should normally be done not more than a month before the court considers the application. Courts should therefore give the applicants a date for the consideration of their application before the medical reports have been filed; we understand that at present some courts are reluctant to do this.

348. For both examinations, the following information should be regarded as an integral part of the medical assessment of the child.

(a) The medical and social history of the natural parents and their families.

(b) An obstetric report on the mother and the baby's neonatal report (particularly relevant in the case of young babies).

(c) Information on the child's care and placements from birth onwards.

(d) Details of any illnesses or medical treatment he may have had.

The person who cares for the child should bring him for the examination to give information about his behaviour and development. At the pre-court examination, the pre-placement report form should be available to the doctor.

349. Doctors who gave evidence stressed that it would be advantageous if examinations were made by a doctor with special training in children's medicine, including its developmental aspects (e.g. paediatricians and those doctors in maternal and child health clinics or in family practice who have special experience and training). We consider that each agency should have a group of experienced doctors available for the examination of children. There may be instances when the skills of other specialists should be used, especially psychiatrists, psychologists and geneticists. We particularly commend consultation with a child psychiatrist where older children are concerned. It was represented to us that no child should be considered unsuitable for placement on purely medical grounds without a second opinion from an experienced paediatrician. We think that few children, however handicapped, should be considered to be unadoptable, if adopters can be found to accept them with a realistic understanding of their future needs, though in practice there are children with severe mental or physical handicaps for whom it would be extremely difficult to find a home.

350. We think that the law should require agencies to arrange a comprehensive pre-placement examination, and that the regulations should prescribe its nature in broad terms but the specific content of the examination should be left to professional practice. We think that the forms drawn up by the Association of British Adoption Agencies are appropriate for use by agencies as the pre-placement form, and we assume that these forms will be reviewed periodically so that they are kept up-to-date. If some other form is used, its adequacy should be considered by the registering authority. There would be an advantage in similar forms being used throughout the country, especially as inter-agency placements are likely to become more common.

351. Since the second examination is provided for the court, we consider that the report should continue to be in a form prescribed in the rules of court. The contents of the report should be such as to enable the court to form a judgment on whether the adoption order will be for the child's welfare

and should cover the child's present state of health, his general development, any medical risk factors which may be present, and the applicants' understanding and acceptance of these factors; it should also state how far the child appears to be thriving in the adoptive home.

352. The present adoption law requires certain specific tests: a serological test for syphilis taken six weeks or later after the child's birth, a urine test for albumen and sugar, and a test for phenylketonuria. An agency is required by the regulations to furnish the proposed adopters with copies of the reports of these tests. Most babies born in this country are now tested efficiently for phenylketonuria, but the doctor must make sure that this has been done. Medical opinion is at present divided on the need for a routine serological test for syphilis. Some doctors consider that it is unnecessary as a routine procedure provided always that the mother has been tested with negative results in the last trimester of pregnancy, and that a comprehensive clinical assessment of the baby is negative. Others consider that the test is still essential in all cases because of the possibility, remote though it may be, of infection late in pregnancy.

353. We are impressed by the view that this test and other specific tests should be left to good practice and we recommend that the Department of Health and Social Security and the Scottish Home and Health Department should periodically review the need for specific tests in the light of advances in medical knowledge. If tests are recommended, it will be necessary for them to be prescribed in the form of the medical report to be sent to the court. The results of any tests carried out at the pre-placement stage should be communicated to the doctor providing the report to the court.

Medical requirements relating to the adopters

354. The existing law requires each applicant for an adoption order to attach to his application a very brief certificate of a fully registered medical practitioner as to his health. There is no requirement for a medical examination as part of the agency's initial enquiries. Again practice has moved ahead of the law and agencies almost invariably take up a medical reference, generally requiring a report of a comprehensive medical history and examination.

355. In general, the evidence supported the suggestion in our working paper that the law should require a comprehensive medical examination of each adoptive applicant as part of the pre-placement study. The purpose of the examination is to ascertain the prospective adopters' health and life expectancy, details of any likely disability, the stability of their marriage and their general emotional adjustment. Medical, psychological and social factors are inter-related and must be considered together, and special attention should be paid to a couple's attitude to their infertility or genetic problems where these are relevant. There was divided opinion among our witnesses on whether this examination should be carried out by the applicants' family doctor or by some independent doctor. We adhere to our original opinion that the report should ordinarily be made by the family doctor since he is in the best position to know the full medical history, and will have reports on any referrals to specialists. The agency's physician should assess these reports and obtain

98

further information from the family doctor or other specialists where necessary. We consider that a follow-up check should be made by the family doctor and a report of this should be submitted to the court with a copy to the agency. As with the child, this examination should be a recent one, not more than a month before the court decides the application and courts should give the applicants a date for consideration of the hearing before the medical report is filed (see paragraph 347).

356. As with the pre-placement examination of the child we do not consider that the form for the first examination of the applicants need be prescribed in detail by the law. We consider that this can be left to agency practice and we think the forms which have been drawn up by the Association of British Adoption Agencies are satisfactory for this purpose. We assume that, like the forms relating to the child, they will be reviewed periodically and kept up-to-date. Where some other form is used its adequacy will need to be considered by the registering authority. We consider that the follow-up report for the court should be prescribed by statutory rules and should be shorter than the original report form. Its purpose is to inform the court fully of any present health problems or risks for the future for each applicant. The court would know that a comprehensive examination of the applicants had been carried out before placement and could ask for more information if it thought this necessary.

Non-agency cases

357. There will continue to be a number of adoption applications where the placement has not been arranged by a registered adoption agency. These will be applications by relatives or foster parents (whether private foster parents or local authority or voluntary child care agency foster parents). We consider that, in these non-agency cases, the report on the child provided for the court would need to be in the same form as that prescribed for the court in agency cases. It would be open to the local authority to require additional medical information or investigation where this seemed advisable. With regard to the applicants we recommend that the local authority should have a duty to ensure that a comprehensive examination is carried out by the family doctor on the lines mentioned in paragraph 355 and that the local authority medical adviser should inspect the report. The report to the court would be shorter and on the same prescribed form as mentioned in paragraph 356.

Medical records and confidentiality

358. Care should be taken to maintain confidentiality in regard to the child's placement, subsequent adoption and change of name, where medical records are concerned. This involves appropriate changes in the family doctor's records, in public health records, and in hospital records, and it is essential that doctors and health visitors should be aware of the importance of accurately recording the changes and safeguarding the confidentiality of the information.

Recommendations

359. A high standard of agency practice in regard to the medical aspects of adoption is essential and the agency's medical arrangements will be among the aspects considered by the registering authority. Where specific legal require-

ments are concerned, *we recommend* that:—

The law should place on agencies, and on local authorities in the case of non-agency placements, a duty to ensure that a comprehensive examination of the child and the adopters is carried out. These examinations should be carried out before placement in the case of agency adoptions. The law should prescribe the nature of the examinations in broad terms, the specific content to be left to professional practice.

(Recommendation 88)

In all cases there should be a recent examination of the child and the applicants for the purpose of reports to the court, the form of which should be prescribed by statutory rules.

(Recommendation 89)

In non-agency placements the medical reports to the court should be in the same form as those prescribed for agency placements.

(Recommendation 90)

The need for the requirement in the law for specific tests, including the test for syphilis, should be periodically reviewed.

(Recommendation 91)

Fees

360. Medical reports for the purpose of adoption are not among those which a doctor is required to issue free of charge under his terms of service with the National Health Service. At present practice varies: some doctors do not charge; in other cases the fee for the pre-placement examination of the child is paid either by the natural parents or the agency; the applicants pay fees for both their examinations and for that of the child after placement. In our working paper we asked for comment on the question whether natural parents and adopters should be relieved of this expense.

361. There was a wide variety of views on this question. There was general agreement that the doctors performing the examination should receive a specific fee (except where medical officers of local authority health clinics examined a child). There was a broad measure of agreement that the natural parents should be relieved of the expense. There was less agreement with regard to the applicants. A substantial minority of those who commented thought that they should continue to pay the cost of their examinations, either to the doctor direct or through the agency. But the majority view was that the applicants, like the natural parent, should be relieved of this expense. The suggested ways of doing so included payment from National Health Service funds, by the central government, by the local authority and by the agency. Some witnesses pointed out that the question is related to that of the financing of the adoption service and to the charging of fees and expenses to applicants (see paragraphs 62 to 67).

362. We approached the Supplementary Benefits Commission to see whether they could help in the case of mothers. The Commission has now agreed that, where a mother giving up her child for adoption is within the scope of the supplementary benefits scheme, and the adoption agency is not a local authority, they will, under their discretionary powers, consider a request for an exceptional needs payment to cover the cost of the medical certificates and reports relating

to the mother and child before the placement. We welcome this helpful con-
cession by the Commission, which we understand has already been put into
effect. But it will benefit only those mothers within the scope of the supplementary benefits scheme.

363. We think that a way should be sought of relieving natural parents and
adopters of these costs. We are influenced by the view that adoption is primarily
a service to children rather than to couples seeking a child. This is particularly
the case now that greater emphasis is being laid on finding adoptive homes for
a much wider variety of children, including children with special needs.
Adoption is a service to the community, and adopters, while achieving personal
fulfilment and satisfaction by adopting a child, are participants in this service.
Some witnesses have suggested that a grant should be made to couples who
adopt a child, analogous to the maternity grant, to help towards the considerable initial cost involved in providing essential equipment. Certainly if the
children concerned were not absorbed into adoptive families they would, in the
majority of cases, remain a liability to the community, not only in the narrow
sense that many would remain in public care, but in the wider sense that some
would be permanently damaged by their deprivation and require rehabilitative
treatment later on.

364. Accordingly, we recommend that the Department of Health and Social
Security should consider ways of relieving natural parents and adopters of the
cost of medical examinations, by enabling this to be met from public funds. We
have been told that there are objections to the cost being met from National
Health Service funds. Again, in regard to the suggestion for a "maternity grant"
to adoptive parents, we understand that there might be difficulty about paying a
social security grant twice in respect of the same child. The arguments we have
put forward in the preceding paragraph suggest that the advantages to society
of adoption, including the financial advantages, far outweigh the cost of a
contribution towards the outlay involved in adopting a child. We think that, in
common with other medical services for children, the cost of both the examinations of the child should certainly be borne by public funds; and in view of the
service rendered to society by adopters, we think there is a strong case for their
examinations also to be free of charge.

Recommendation

365. Accordingly *we recommend* that:—

The Department of Health and Social Security should devise a way of
meeting from public funds the cost of the medical examinations of the
child and, in view of the service rendered to society by adopters, should
also consider relieving them of the cost of their examinations.

(Recommendation 92)

LIST OF RECOMMENDATIONS

1 The law should continue to provide for the adoption of children.
(Paragraph 30)

2 The law should place on local authorities a duty to provide an adoption service as part of their general child care and family casework provision.
(Paragraph 42)

3 Local authorities should have a statutory duty to ensure, in co-operation with voluntary societies, that a comprehensive adoption service is available throughout their area.

(Paragraphs 40–43)

4 The central government professional advisory and consultancy services should be available to all voluntary adoption societies.
(Paragraphs 46–47)

5 Responsibility for registering voluntary adoption societies should rest with the Secretary of State.
(Paragraphs 51–55)

6 Registration should be renewable every three years.
(Paragraph 59)

7 The Secretary of State should have power to call for information and to cancel registration.
(Paragraph 59)

8 Criteria should be prescribed which are relevant to the programme, resources and organisation of voluntary societies.
(Paragraphs 56–58)

9 Agencies should remain free to charge expenses and to accept contributions towards the cost of arranging adoptions.
(Paragraphs 62–65)

10 Local authorities should make realistic financial arrangements with voluntary adoption societies participating in the provision of the adoption service in their areas and make contributions towards the work of the societies which bear some relation to the actual costs incurred.
(Paragraph 66)

11 The basic legal conditions of eligibility to adopt a child should cover the domicile, residence, minimum age and marital status of the adopters. The minimum age should be 21 years. The prohibition in section 2(3) of the 1958 Act should be repealed.
(Paragraphs 70–78)

12 The information which agencies should obtain about prospective adopters should no longer be prescribed by law.

(Paragraph 79)

13 The law should make it an offence for a person other than an adoption agency to place a child with a person who is not a relative (as defined in the 1958 Act) for the purpose of adoption.

(Paragraphs 84–90)

14 The law should make it an offence for a person who is not a relative (as defined in the 1958 Act) to receive a child for the purpose of adoption otherwise than through an adoption agency registered in this country.

(Paragraphs 84–90)

15 The law should require an applicant for an adoption order, who is not a relative, to have cared for the child for twelve months or more if the child was not placed with him by an adoption agency.

(Paragraph 91)

16 Recommendations 13 to 15 should be brought into effect once the new registration system is in force and agencies are registered under the new system.

17 The law should be amended to permit pilot schemes of payment of allowances to adopters under the general oversight of the Secretary of State.

(Paragraphs 93–94)

18 The law should require the court to be satisfied that there are special circumstances which justify as an exceptional measure the making of an order in favour of a natural parent alone, and these circumstances should be recorded by the court.

(Paragraphs 98–102)

19 An adoption order granted to the natural mother alone should terminate any obligation of the putative father to make payments in respect of the child under an affiliation order, or decree of affiliation and aliment, or agreement, in the same way as does an adoption order granted to any other person.

(Paragraph 102)

20 In the light of recommendation 21 (that relatives caring for a child should be able to apply for guardianship), where a relative (including a step-parent applying jointly with his spouse) applies to adopt a child, the law should require the court first to consider whether guardianship would be more appropriate in all the circumstances of the case, first consideration being given to the long-term welfare of the child.

(Paragraphs 107–114)

21 The right to apply for custody under the Guardianship of Minors Act 1971 (which we call, for convenience, "guardianship") should be extended for

this purpose to relatives already caring for a child and foster parents, but it should not be open to foster parents to apply until they have cared for the child for at least twelve months.

(Paragraphs 120–122)

22 A guardianship order should not deprive the natural parents of the right to consent, or withhold consent, to adoption. Subject to this, it should give the guardian parental powers and obligations, but the court should have the power to make an order for access by the parents, and to make a maintenance order where appropriate.

(Paragraph 123)

23 When guardians are appointed by a court for a child in the care of a local authority or voluntary organisation, he should thereby cease to be in their care, and any court order committing him to care or resolution assuming parental rights should lapse on the making of the guardianship order.

(Paragraph 124)

24 Applicants should be required to notify the local authority of their intention to apply for guardianship, and an order should not be made until at least three months have elapsed from the date of notification. The local authority should investigate the circumstances and furnish a report to the court.

(Paragraph 128)

25 The child's parents, the local authority, and any other interested person or body, should be a party to such a guardianship application, with a right to be heard before the court takes its decision.

(Paragraph 125)

26 The powers of the courts in dealing with guardianship applications should include, in exceptional circumstances, power to make a supervision order whether or not it grants the application, and to commit the child to the care of the local authority on refusing the application.

(Paragraph 129)

27 Parents should have the right to apply at any time for the revocation of a guardianship order so that the child may return to them, but the court should have discretion not to proceed with such applications if they are made repeatedly where there has been no change in circumstances.

(Paragraphs 131–132)

28 A local authority should have power to apply for a revocation or variation of a guardianship order in respect of a child received into its care.

(Paragraph 133)

29 Local authorities should have power to pay allowances to persons who are granted guardianship orders if there is a need for financial assistance.

(Paragraphs 134–136)

30 An explanatory leaflet should be given to the parents of every child received into care.

(Paragraph 151)

31 The law should require 28 days' notice of removal of a child who has been in the care of a local authority for 12 months or more, and during this period of notice it should not be possible to remove the child without the permission of the caring authority.

(Paragraph 152)

32 Local authorities should have discretion to resolve to assume parental rights over any child who has been in their care for three years. If such a decision were challenged, the court should be required to consider not only whether the three years period had elapsed, but also whether the continuation of the resolution would be in the child's welfare.

(Paragraph 156)

33 The grounds for assumption of parental rights should be extended to protect children where rights may be assumed in respect of one parent and not the other.

(Paragraph 157)

34 Local authorities should have power to assume parental rights in respect of children in the care of a voluntary society, if the society so requests.

(Paragraph 158)

35 There should be a right of appeal from the decision of a juvenile court to uphold a resolution assuming parental rights.

(Paragraph 159)

36 Where foster parents who have cared for a child for five years or more apply for an adoption or guardianship order, the natural parents should not be able to remove the child before the hearing without the leave of the court.

(Paragraph 164)

37 Relinquishment and transfer of parental rights should require the approval of a court, on an application made jointly by the parent and an adoption agency.

(Paragraph 173)

38 The court should be required to be satisfied that the mother, after considering the alternatives and implications, had freely decided to relinquish parental rights.

(Paragraph 173)

39 The court hearing a relinquishment application should have power to proceed in the absence of the mother and accept written evidence of her decision to relinquish parental rights.

(Paragraph 180)

40 Written evidence of her decision should be witnessed by a social worker appointed by the court, known as the reporting officer, who would have a duty to furnish the court with a report on whether the mother had freely made her decision after considering the alternatives and implications.

(Paragraphs 176–177)

41 The rights and interests of any other person or body (e.g. a putative father or a local authority having care of the child) should be considered before an order transferring parental rights was made.

(Paragraph 173)

42 If satisfied that the mother had freely decided to relinquish parental rights, with a full understanding of its implications and the alternatives, the court should make an order vesting all parental rights in the agency, who would retain them until an adoption order was made.

(Paragraph 173)

43 The transfer of parental rights should be irrevocable, subject to the right of the mother to ask to be notified if no adoption order was made within twelve months and, in that case, to apply to the court for parental rights to be restored, unless an adoption application was then before the court. If no such application was made by the mother the agency would retain the rights and obligations until the child's majority or until they were transferred by court order, or transferred to some other local authority or agency by agreement approved by the court.

(Paragraphs 184–185)

44 The agency to which parental rights had been transferred should have the power to consent to an adoption order on producing the order of the court which had transferred parental rights.

(Paragraph 170)

45 Consent to a specific adoption application should become final, as at present, when an adoption order was made, the mother being a respondent to the adoption application. A reporting officer would be appointed who would witness the mother's written consent and make a report to the court.

(Paragraph 187)

46 The period before which the mother cannot give consent to adoption should remain six weeks so long as the European Convention on Adoption so provides. The same minimum period should apply to the written statement of willingness to relinquish parental rights made before the reporting officer.

(Paragraphs 188–190)

47 The putative father's right to apply for custody should remain.

(Paragraph 193)

48 In relinquishment proceedings the putative father's interests should be finally determined at that stage; if he has been concerned in the child's upbringing and maintenance he should be made a respondent to a

relinquishment application; but if he is not known, cannot be found or fails to appear, then freeing of the child for adoption should not be delayed.

(Paragraphs 194–196)

49 Once parental rights have been transferred to an agency the right of the putative father to apply for custody should be terminated, together with his obligation to pay maintenance under an affiliation order, or decree of affiliation and aliment, or an agreement.

(Paragraph 196)

50 Where there is a relinquishment application the position of the mother's husband should be considered at that stage. If the mother states that her husband is not the father, the court should not notify the husband of the relinquishment application until it has heard any evidence brought on behalf of the mother to support her statement. If the mother fails to satisfy the court that her husband is not the father, yet wishes to continue with the application, she should be informed that the proceedings cannot continue unless the husband joins her as an applicant.

(Paragraphs 199–202)

51 The statute law should provide that, in deciding whether a parent is withholding consent to adoption unreasonably, the court shall have regard to all the circumstances, first consideration being given to the effect of the parent's decision on the long-term welfare of the child.

(Paragraphs 205–217)

52 An additional ground on which the court should be empowered to dispense with the consent of a parent to adoption should be that the parent has seriously ill-treated the child and the court is satisfied that the rehabilitation of the child in the family is unlikely.

(Paragraph 219)

53 The law should enable a local authority or registered adoption society to apply to a court for the transfer of parental rights over a child in their care to the agency with a view to the child's adoption and for the parents' consent to adoption to be dispensed with on one of the statutory grounds. The law should prevent the removal of the child by a parent pending the hearing.

(Paragraphs 221–224)

54 Rules of court should require a person who intends to ask any court to dispense with a parent's consent to adoption to furnish the court, and the parent, in advance of the hearing, with a statement of the matters on which he intends to rely.

(Paragraph 226)

55 It should cease to be possible to give consent to adoption subject to a condition as to the religious persuasion in which the child is to be brought up.

(Paragraphs 228–230)

56 Adoption orders should continue to be made by courts.
(Paragraph 232)

57 The agency which has placed the child should be responsible for the supervision of the child in the adoptive home, and for helping and advising the adopters throughout the period between the placement and the court hearing. Accordingly, welfare supervision of the child by the local authority, and the requirement to notify the local authority of the intention to apply for an adoption order, should be discontinued in agency cases once the new registration scheme has come into operation. The existing requirements for notification to the local authority and for welfare supervision should continue in non-agency cases.
(Paragraphs 237–240)

58 The minimum period for which the applicants must have cared for the child before an adoption order can be granted should remain three months, not counting the first six weeks of the child's life.
(Paragraph 241)

59 Courts should have discretion to grant an order to joint applicants resident overseas where the period of care and possession in Great Britain by one of the applicants falls outside the three months immediately preceding the date of the order.
(Paragraph 243)

60 The agency should be accountable to the court, making a full written report direct to the court, being a party to the proceedings, and being represented at the hearing.
(Paragraph 244)

61 In both relinquishment and adoption applications the appointment of a guardian ad litem or curator ad litem should be at the discretion of the court.
(Paragraphs 246–252)

62 The duties of a guardian or curator ad litem should be carried out by social workers, appointed from a list approved by the courts. The court should have discretion to order that the guardian should be legally represented at public expense.
(Paragraphs 254–255)

63 None of the recommendations 57 to 62 made in Chapter 9 should be brought into force until the new registration procedure is in operation.
(Paragraph 256)

64 Adoption proceedings in magistrates' courts should be transferred from the juvenile court to the domestic court and arrangements should be made for the selection of suitable magistrates to sit in that court.
(Paragraph 263)

65 The rules which limit applications to courts in the applicants' or child's home area should be relaxed.
(Paragraph 264)

66 There should be power for the courts to summon expert witnesses if they consider this desirable, and the cost should be met from public funds.

(Paragraph 265)

67 Courts should have discretion whether to require the applicants for an adoption order to attend a hearing.

(Paragraphs 266–268)

68 Legal aid should be available to all the parties at all stages in adoption proceedings where there is a dispute. Legal Aid Committees should consider more readily the granting of emergency certificates in adoption proceedings.

(Paragraphs 271–272)

69 Courts at all levels should be aware of the need to avoid delay in hearing adoption cases. In the case of an appeal it should be possible to apply to the court whose decision is being appealed against for a certificate that the case is one of urgency.

(Paragraphs 273–274)

70 Adoption jurisdiction at first instance in Scotland should remain with the sheriff court and the Court of Session, but should be transferred from the Inner to the Outer House of the latter court.

(Paragraphs 283–286)

71 The court in Scotland should be empowered, either on its own motion, or on the joint motion of the parties, or—with its agreement—on the motion of one party, to appoint expert assessors to assist in the weighing up of evidence. Where expert assessors are required they should be chosen in consultation with the professional organisations concerned, and the cost should be met from public funds.

(Paragraphs 287–290)

72 It should be within the discretion of the Scottish court to decide whether there should be a hearing for adoption applications or applications for guardianship by relatives or foster parents. Whether there is a hearing or not, there should be adequate contact between the sheriff and the adoption agency or curator.

(Paragraphs 291–292)

73 Recommendation No. 69 (avoidance of delay) should apply to Scotland.

(Paragraph 293)

74 Natural parents who relinquish their children for adoption should be able to be anonymous so far as the adopters are concerned.

(Paragraphs 297–298)

75 The adoption agency or, where there is no agency, the local authority, should be named on the adoption order.

(Paragraph 299)

76 Arrangements should be made for the preservation of adoption records for 75 years.

(Paragraph 299)

77 An adopted person aged 18 years or over should be entitled to a copy of his original birth certificate.

(Paragraphs 302–303)

78 Courts should have discretion to grant or refuse an application from an adopted person for the disclosure of information from the court records of the adoption proceedings.

(Paragraph 305)

79 Where a court refuses an application for an adoption order it should have discretion to extend the period for the return of the child to the agency up to a maximum of six weeks.

(Paragraph 307)

80 Where a court refuses an application for an adoption order in non-agency cases, it should have power to make an alternative order, i.e. a supervision order or an order committing the child to the care of the local authority.

(Paragraph 308)

81 There should be a right of appeal against an interim order made by any court.

(Paragraph 310)

82 The power to make provisional adoption orders should remain, but there should be improvements in practice and the form of such orders should be redrafted.

(Paragraphs 317–319)

83 An adopted child should have exactly the same rights under wills and other instruments as a natural child of the adoptive family.

(Paragraphs 326–327)

84 The present prohibitions on marriage should not be extended.

(Paragraphs 329–332)

85 All agencies should have established machinery for making decisions.

(Paragraphs 335–336)

86 Policy decisions will normally be taken by the controlling committee, which could include both lay members and professional workers. Case decisions should always be group decisions, either by a professional group or a mixed professional and lay group.

(Paragraphs 337–339)

87 Casework should not be undertaken by committee members who are not professional social workers.

(Paragraph 338)

88 The law should place on agencies, and on local authorities in the case of non-agency placements, a duty to ensure that a comprehensive examination of the child and the adopters is carried out. These examinations should be carried out before placement in the case of agency adoptions. The law should prescribe the nature of the examinations in broad terms, the specific content to be left to professional practice.

(Paragraph 350)

89 In all cases there should be a recent examination of the child and the applicants for the purpose of reports to the court, the form of which should be prescribed by statutory rules.

(Paragraphs 347,
351,
355
and 356)

90 In non-agency placements the medical reports to the court should be in the same form as those prescribed for agency placements.

(Paragraph 357)

91 The need for the requirement in the law for specific tests, including the test for syphilis, should be periodically reviewed.

(Paragraphs 352–353)

92 The Department of Health and Social Security should devise a way of meeting from public funds the cost of the medical examinations of the child and, in view of the service rendered to society by adopters, should also consider relieving them of the cost of their examinations.

(Paragraphs 363–364)

F A STOCKDALE
LEO ABSE
W K ANGUS
MARGARET BRAMALL
W J BRYDEN
CHRISTINE E COOPER
IRIS GOODACRE
HILARY HALPIN
PHILIP HARVEY

PHILIP HUGHES
JANET T LUSK
EVELYN M MAGNESS
JANE ROWE
F W STONE
JOAN VICKERS
D T WHITE

MURIEL M PECK ⎫ JOINT SECRETARIES
PATRICIA ROBERTS ⎭

24 July 1972

PUBLICATIONS REFERRED TO IN THE TEXT

(For a complete bibliography of adoption publications see Kellmer Pringle ML, *Adoption—Facts and Fallacies*, Longmans (London) 1967, and Jacka A *Adoption in Brief. An Annotated Bibliography (1966–72)*, National Foundation for Educational Research, (London) 1972.)

[1] Grey E, in collaboration with Blunden RM, *A Survey of Adoption in Great Britain*, HM Stationery Office, (Home Office Research Studies No. 10) (London) 1971.

[2] Seglow J, Kellmer Pringle ML and Wedge P, *Growing Up Adopted*, National Foundation for Educational Research, (London) 1972.

[3] A Guide to Adoption Practice, Advisory Council on Child Care, No. 2, HM Stationery Office (London) 1970.

[4] Adoption of Children, Departmental Committee on the Adoption of Children, HM Stationery Office (London) 1970.

[5] Raynor L, *Giving up a baby for adoption*, Association of British Adoption Agencies (London) 1971.

[6] Triseliotis J and Hall E, *Giving consent to adoption*, Social Work Today, 2 December 1971.

[7] Triseliotis J, *In Search of Origins*, to be published by Routledge and Kegan Paul, 1973.

[8] Report of the Departmental Committee on the Adoption of Children, HM Stationery Office, (Cmd 9248), (London) 1954.

[9] Report of the Committee on Child Adoption, HM Stationery Office, (Cmd 1254) (London) 1921.

[10] Child Adoption Committee First Report, HM Stationery Office, (Cmd 2401) (London) 1925.

[11] Child Adoption Committee Second Report, HM Stationery Office, (Cmd 2469) (London) 1925.

[12] Report of the Departmental Committee on Adoption Societies and Agencies, HM Stationery Office, (Cmd 5499) (London) 1937.

[13] Final Act of Tenth Session of The Hague Conference on Private International Law, October 1964, Convention on jurisdiction, applicable law and recognition of decrees relating to adoptions, HM Stationery Office, (Cmnd 2613) (London) 1965.

[14] Home Office Report on the Work of the Children's Department 1967–1969, HM Stationery Office, (London) 1970.

[15] Crellin E, Kellmer Pringle M L, West P, *Born Illegitimate* a report by the National Children's Bureau, National Foundation for Educational Research, (London) 1971.

[16] Raynor L, *Adoption of non-white children*, George Allen and Unwin Ltd (London) 1970.

[17] International Social Service of Great Britain, Annual Report for 1971.

[18] Jaffee B and Fanshel D, *How they fared in adoption*, Studies of the Child Welfare League of America, Columbia University Press, 1970.

[19] Lewis H, *Deprived Children*, Oxford University Press, 1954.

[20] Kadushin A, *Adopting Older Children*, Columbia University Press, New York, 1970.

[21] Chester R, Divorce in the Nineteen Sixties, Marriage Guidance, Vol. 14, No. 2, March 1972.

[22] Report of the Committee on Legal Education (Cmnd 4595) (London) 1971.

[23] Case Committees and Organisation, Child Adoption, 68, No. 2 of 1972.

APPENDIX A

ORGANISATIONS WHICH GAVE WRITTEN AND ORAL EVIDENCE—WITH THE NAMES OF WITNESSES

Adoption Resource Exchange
  Mrs M M Carriline
  Miss P Sawbridge

Adoptive Parents' Association
  Mr B Edwards
  Mr P Glynn

Association of British Adoption Agencies
  The Reverend J Dunne
  Mr J Llewellyn
  Miss E Palmer
  Mr A Rampton OBE (Chairman)

Association of British Adoption Agencies (Scottish Group)
  Mrs K McGarry
  Mr W Y McNeil

Association of British Adoption Agencies (Medical Group)
  Dr F N Bamford
  Dr J Marshall
  Dr J Price

Association of Child Care Officers
  Mr C Andrews
  Mr G Chown
  Mr J W D Davies

Association of County Councils in Scotland
  Mr A A L Evans
  Miss M C Faulds
  Lt Col F R N Kerr
  Mr D A McDonald
  Mr G H Spiers (Deputy Secretary)

Association of Directors of Social Work (Scotland)
  Mr S H Johnston
  Miss M Urquhart

Association of Municipal Corporations
  Miss L Faithfull
  Mr W Hopkin
  Mr E B Roycroft
  Mr R R Thornton
  Mrs J M White

Bar Council
  Mr M Astbury (Assistant Secretary)
  Mr L Blom Cooper QC
  Mr J Jackson QC
  Mr G Rodway

British Association of Social Workers
  Mr C Andrews
  Mr K Bilton (Assistant Secretary)
  Miss C Pollock
  Miss S Poupard
  Mrs J Thomas

British Association of Social Workers (Scottish Region)
  Miss V Lobban
  Mrs E Mapstone
  'Mrs J Stronach

British Medical Association
  Dr I T Field (Assistant Secretary)
  Dr C D L Lycett
  Dr B Wolman

British Psycho-Analytical Society
  Dr A Davidson
  Dr S Isaacs
  Dr C Yorke

British Psychological Society
  Mr R M Farr (General Secretary)
  Mr M Humphrey
  Miss G Keir
  Dr T Lee

Chancery Masters
  Chief Master Ball
  Master Chamberlain

Church of England Children's Society
  The Reverend R C M Beeny (General Secretary)
  Miss W Stone

Church of Scotland Committee on Social Service
  Miss M R Campbell
  Miss M G Combe
  The Reverend W F Grieve (Senior Vice-Convenor)

County Councils Association
  Mr L W K Brown (Deputy Secretary)
  Miss D E Harvie
  Mr W R Scurfield

Dr Barnardo's
  Dr N Bywaters
  Mr E Ingram
  Miss D Warren
  Mrs J Young

Guild of Service, Edinburgh
  Mrs J G M Hamilton
  Miss K J Hines
  Mrs J Rae
  Miss R C Williamson

115

International Social Service of Great Britain
  Mr P Archer QC MP
  Mrs W Klingender
  Miss W I Rouse (Director)

Justices' Clerks' Society
  Mr J D Berryman
  Mr J B Horsman (Honorary Secretary)
  Mr W Scott

Law Society
  Mr C Clarke
  Mr G A MacDonald
  Mr B Passingham
  Mr D Rubery DFC
  Mr M T Sennett (Assistant Secretary)

Law Society of Scotland
  Mr C Brown
  Mr K G Macgregor
  Mr R M Webster (Deputy Secretary)

Magistrates' Association
  Mr A J Brayshaw OBE JP (Secretary)
  Mrs W E Cavenagh JP
  Mr L Goodman

Mothers in Action
  Miss J Hunton

National Association of Probation Officers
  Mr T Bales
  Mrs A M Martyr

National Society for the Prevention of Cruelty to Children
  Mr L G Bennett
  Mrs J Moore
  The Reverend A Morton OBE (Director)

Official Solicitor
  Mr N H Turner

Registrar General for Scotland
  Mr R MacLeod (Deputy Registrar General)
  Mr D Baird

Royal College of General Practitioners
  Dr E V Kuenssberg OBE
  Dr N C Mond

Royal College of Obstetricians and Gynaecologists
  Dr E A J Alment
  Miss J Barnes

Royal Medico-Psychological Association
  Dr L A Hersov
  Dr A C Woodmansey

116

Sheriffs—Substitute Association
  Sheriff J Aikman Smith
  Sheriff J S Mowat (Honorary Secretary)

Society of Medical Officers of Health
  Dr J D Kershaw
  Dr B M Thompson

Thomas Coram Foundation
  Miss E M Marshall

West Midlands Foster Parents' Association
  Mrs B Bond
  Mrs J Crockett
  Mr D Guest (Chairman)

ORAL EVIDENCE ONLY

American Bar Association
  Judge Burdick
  Mr Felix Infausto
  Professor Katz
  Mr F O'Connell
  Mrs E R Sheps
  Judge Zuckerman

INDIVIDUALS WHO GAVE WRITTEN AND ORAL EVIDENCE

Mr L Blom Cooper QC
Mrs Mollie Bowen
Mr J M Eekelaar   University of Oxford
Dr V George   }   University of Nottingham
Miss Rachel Jenkins
His Honour Judge F K Glazebrook
His Honour Judge H B Grant
His Honour Judge Rowe Harding
Miss D E Harvie   }   Kent Children's Department
Miss B C Reid

Miss Margaret Kornitzer
Dr Alexina McWhinnie
Mr D H Parkinson
Dr M L Kellmer Pringle   National Children's Bureau
Miss Lois Raynor
Mr P Schofield   University of Leeds
His Honour Judge D Stinson
Dr J P Triseliotis   University of Edinburgh
Dame Eileen Younghusband

ORAL EVIDENCE ONLY

Dr J Bowlby

OTHER ORGANISATIONS AND INDIVIDUALS
WHO SUBMITTED WRITTEN EVIDENCE

Adoption Societies:
  Doncaster and District Adoption Society
  Independent Adoption Society
  Lancashire and Cheshire Child Adoption Council
  Lancaster Diocesan Protection and Rescue Society
  Lincoln Diocesan Board for Social Work
Advisory Council on Child Care (England and Wales)
Advisory Council on Social Work (Scotland)
Association of Children's Officers
Association of Child Psychotherapists (non medical)
Association of County Court Registrars
Association of Directors of Social Service
Association of Head Mistresses

British Association of Social Workers:
  North of Scotland Group
  Croydon and East Surrey Branch
  Nottingham and Nottinghamshire Branch
British Humanist Association

Church of England Board for Social Responsibility
Cobden Trust and National Council for Civil Liberties
Commission for Social Welfare
Convention of Royal Burghs
Council of County Court Judges
Councils of Social Service:
  Birmingham
  Cumberland
  Woking
Counties of Cities Association
Court of the Chief Rabbi

Department of Health and Social Security
Devon Adopters' Groups

Faculty of Advocates
Free Church Federal Council

Health Visitors' Association
Home Office Children's Inspectorate

Institute of Medical Social Workers:
  The Maternity Group
  Glasgow and District
Institute of Psychiatry

Local Authorities:
  Hertfordshire County Council
  Lancashire County Council
  Wiltshire County Council
  London Borough of Camden
  London Borough of Greenwich
  Birmingham City Council

Medical Women's Federation
Mothers' Union

National Association for Mental Health
National Board of Catholic Women
National Federation of Women's Institutes
National Secular Society
National Council for the Unmarried Mother and her Child

President of the Probate, Divorce and Admiralty Division of the High Court
Public Record Office

Registrar General for England and Wales
Religious Society of Friends
Royal College of Midwives
Royal College of Nursing
Royal College of General Practitioners—Scottish Council
Royal College of Physicians of Edinburgh
Royal Scottish Society for Prevention of Cruelty to Children

Salvation Army
Scottish Council for the Unmarried Mother and her Child
Scottish Law Agents' Society
Sheriff Clerks' Association
Standing Conference of Principal Probation Officers
Stockport and District Catholic Committee

University of Liverpool—Postgraduate Social Science Students

Wives' Group of Christ the King Church, Bromborough
Women's National Commission

Mr Christopher Bagley
Dr Frank Bamford
Alderman C Barcroft
Mrs Gwen Belcher
Mr Thomas Bennett
Miss Elizabeth Birch
Mrs Mary Buckfield
Mrs Morag Butcher
Miss Jessie Butler

Mrs Jean Chadwick
Mr and Mrs David Chambers
Mrs Joanna Clark
Mr Felix Crowder

Mr Stephen Edell
Mr R C Edwards
Dr Louise Eickhoff
Mrs Elizabeth Evans JP
Mr H J Ballinger JP
Professor U F J Eyck

Professor J O Forfar
Mrs M Francis

His Honour Judge J Garrard
Dr J C Gibbins
Mr L C B Gower
Miss Audrey Gray
Mr David Green

Mr David Hadfield
Mr John Hepperman
Mr Richard Hines
Miss Janet Hitchman
Mr Leonard Huglin
Mr C R Humphery-Smith
Mr Michael Humphrey

Miss Eira Johnson
Mr Richard Joyce

Mr David Lang
Mr A E Leeding
His Honour Judge E Daly Lewis

Miss Carol Mathison
Mrs A J Mole

Mr and Mrs Robert Neighbour
Mrs Elizabeth Newby
Mrs Caroline Nicholson
Mr Donald Norman-Goodhew
Mrs Doris Francis

Miss J M Oldfield
Mr T C O'Toole

Mr and Mrs R F Partridge
Mr A Laurance Polak
Mr John Pottinger
Mrs Rose Post
Mr J Preece
The Reverend Ilex Pullenayegum

Mr H H Radford

Mr Alec Samuels
Mr Bryan Shepherd
Dr Faith Spicer JP
Mr and Mrs Alan Stain
Dr Olive Stone

Mr Michael Tinne
Miss Ethel Tollemache
Mr Antony Tuck
Mr Theodore F Tucker OBE

Mrs E Ward
Mr and Mrs Kenneth Warr
Mrs S Wilkinson
His Honour Judge Bazil Wingate-Saul

APPENDIX B

STATISTICS OF ADOPTION ORDERS

TABLE 1

Year (1)	England and Wales				Scotland	Grand Total (7)
	High Court (2)	County Courts (3)	Juvenile Courts (4)	Total (5)	(6)	
1927	133	184	2,626	2,943	—	2,943
1928	124	236	2,918	3,278	—	3,278
1929	72	224	2,998	3,294	—	3,294
1930	74	317	4,120	4,511	3	4,514
1931	68	274	3,777	4,119	347	4,466
1932	38	264	4,163	4,465	492	4,957
1933	61	262	4,201	4,524	437	4,961
1934	45	290	4,421	4,756	602	5,358
1935	64	342	4,438	4,844	683	5,527
1936	62	372	4,746	5,180	704	5,884
1937	78	413	5,056	5,547	820	6,367
1938	85	446	5,662	6,193	812	7,005
1939	65	635	6,126	6,826	1,100	7,926
1940	59	645	7,071	7,775	1,424	9,199
1941	44	709	6,676	7,429	1,222	8,651
1942	55	1,153	9,201	10,409	1,563	11,972
1943	57	1,504	9,987	11,548	1,747	13,295
1944	58	1,928	11,041	13,027	1,681	14,708
1945	52	2,622	13,645	16,319	1,876	18,195
1946	166	3,815	17,291	21,272	2,292	23,564
1947	183	3,663	14,409	18,255	1,890	20,145
1948	170	3,962	14,408	18,540	2,073	20,613
1949	199	4,337	12,781	17,317	1,764	19,081
1950	152	3,448	9,139	12,739	1,289	14,028
1951	114	3,757	9,979	13,850	1,562	15,412
1952	74	4,280	9,540	13,894	1,523	15,417
1953	75	4,297	8,623	12,995	1,486	14,481
1954	56	4,529	8,418	13,003	1,343	14,346
1955	73	4,791	8,137	13,001	1,352	14,353
1956	44	5,118	8,036	13,198	1,358	14,556
1957	44	5,553	7,804	13,401	1,405	14,806
1958	53	5,899	7,351	13,303	1,365	14,668
1959	46 (1)	6,529 (70)	7,530	14,105 (71)	1,236 (–)	15,341 (71)
1960	42 (2)	7,602 (205)	7,455	15,099 (207)	1,457 (3)	16,556 (210)
1961	55 (1)	8,678 (248)	7,264	15,997 (249)	1,609 (7)	17,606 (256)
1962	53 (4)	9,572 (276)	7,269	16,894 (280)	1,621 (5)	18,515 (285)
1963	74 (–)	10,443 (196)	7,265	17,782 (196)	1,683 (23)	19,465 (219)
1964	59 (1)	12,796 (231)	7,557	20,412 (232)	1,945 (17)	22,357 (249)
1965	55 (–)	13,499 (171)	7,479	21,033 (171)	2,018 (29)	23,051 (200)
1966	50 (–)	14,880 (127)	7,862	22,792 (127)	2,040 (21)	24,832 (148)
1967	45 (1)	15,086 (172)	7,671	22,802 (173)	2,140 (16)	24,942 (189)
1968	39 (4)	16,499 (185)	8,293	24,831 (189)	2,155 (8)	26,986 (197)
1969	31 (2)	15,623 (171)	8,051	23,705 (173)	2,268 (13)	25,973 (186)
1970	16 (1)	14,506 (154)	7,851	22,373 (155)	2,040 (18)	24,413 (173)
1971	40 (–)	13,619 (123)	7,836	21,495 (123)	1,904 (12)	23,399 (135)
Totals	3,302	229,601	348,172	581,075	60,331	641,406

Note:
A very small number of orders are in respect of more than one child, so that the number of children adopted is slightly higher than the number of orders made.

In Scotland, apart from a few orders made by the Court of Session, all orders have been made by Sheriff Courts.

Provisional adoption orders, which were introduced on 1 April 1959 (under Section 53 of the 1958 Act) are included in the totals and shown separately in brackets.

122

ADOPTIONS BY NATURAL PARENTS

TABLE 3

Year	Total number of adoptions	Total number of children adopted by their own parent(s)	Legitimate children		Illegitimate children	
			Joint adopters one or both a parent of the child	Sole adopter a parent of the child	Joint adopters one or both a parent of the child	Sole adopter a parent of the child
England and Wales						
1962	16,894	4,369	1,585	4	2,674	106
1963	17,782	4,651	1,888	11	2,636	116
1964	20,412	5,322	2,291	5	2,951	75
1965	21,033	5,784	2,522	2	3,173	87
1966	22,792	6,898	3,097	27	3,679	95
1967	22,802	7,189	3,090	8	3,963	128
1968	24,831	8,647	4,038	12	4,479	118
1969	23,705	9,335	4,558	11	4,649	117
1970	22,373	10,361	5,202	10	5,054	95
1971	21,495	10,751	5,481	5	5,204	61
Scotland						
1962	1,621	261	45	—	211	5
1963	1,683	297	85	—	211	1
1964	1,945	335	116	1	205	13
1965	2,018	318	98	—	212	8
1966	2,040	364	116	—	246	2
1967	2,140	388	122	—	263	3
1968	2,155	380	137	—	235	8
1969	2,268	458	210	1	242	5
1970	2,040	488	227	—	256	5
1971	1,904	477	209	—	263	5

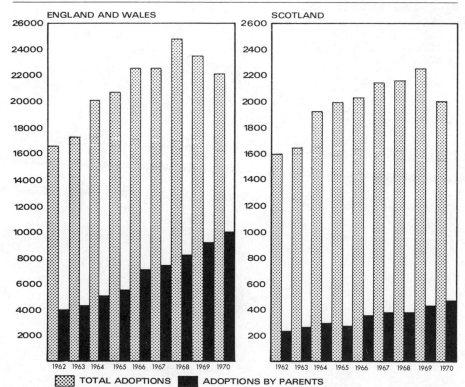

ENGLAND AND WALES   SCOTLAND

▒ TOTAL ADOPTIONS   ■ ADOPTIONS BY PARENTS

PLACEMENTS MADE BY VOLUNTARY SOCIETIES AND LOCAL AUTHORITIES 1966 TO 1971

Voluntary Societies*

TABLE 4

Year	England and Wales	Scotland	Total
1966	8,777	794	9,571
1967	9,101	720	9,821
1968	8,482	739	9,221
1969	7,105	678	7,783
1970	5,911	606	6,517
1971	5,078	562	5,640

Local Authorities†

Year ending 31 March	England and Wales	Scotland	Total
1966	3,203	703	3,906
1967	3,338	754	4,092
1968	3,622	829	4,451
1969	3,600	782	4,382
1970	3,440	799	4,239
1971	3,384	746	4,130

* Taken from informal annual returns made by members of the Association of British Adoption Agencies. The figures are approximate. Some returns do not relate to the year ending 31 December.

† Taken from annual returns made to the Department of Health and Social Security (formerly to the Home Office) and the Scottish Education Department.

ACTUAL LIVE BIRTHS—LEGITIMATE AND ILLEGITIMATE 1955 TO 1971

TABLE 5

Year	Total	Legitimate	Illegitimate	Illegitimate births per 1,000 total live births
England and Wales				
1955	667,811	636,666	31,145	47
1956	700,335	666,801	33,534	48
1957	723,381	688,819	34,562	48
1958	740,715	704,541	36,174	49
1959	748,501	710,340	38,161	51
1960	785,005	742,298	42,707	54
1961	811,281	762,791	48,490	60
1962	838,736	783,360	55,376	66
1963	854,055	794,951	59,104	69
1964	875,972	812,632	63,340	72
1965	862,725	796,476	66,249	77
1966	849,823	782,767	67,056	79
1967	832,164	762,236	69,928	84
1968	819,272	749,466	69,806	85
1969	797,538	730,497	67,041	84
1970	784,486	719,712	64,774	83
1971	783,153	717,475	65,678	84
Scotland				
1955	92,539	88,548	3,991	43
1956	95,313	91,244	4,069	43
1957	97,977	93,960	4,017	41
1958	99,481	95,408	4,073	41
1959	99,251	95,117	4,134	42
1960	101,292	96,883	4,409	44
1961	101,169	96,521	4,648	46
1962	104,334	99,314	5,020	48
1963	102,691	97,351	5,340	52
1964	104,355	98,727	5,628	54
1965	100,660	94,777	5,883	58
1966	96,536	90,376	6,160	64
1967	96,221	89,558	6,663	69
1968	94,786	87,788	6,998	74
1969	90,290	83,563	6,727	75
1970	87,335	80,623	6,712	77
1971	86,731	79,703	7,028	81

ILLEGITIMATE MATERNITIES/LIVE BIRTHS AND PRE-MARITALLY CONCEIVED LEGITIMATE MATERNITIES/LIVE BIRTHS 1955 TO 1970

TABLE 6

Year	Illegitimate maternities/ live births	Pre-maritally conceived legitimate maternities/ live births*	Total maternities/ live births conceived extra-maritally	Percentage of extra-maritally conceived births where the parents married before birth of child
England and Wales				
		Maternities		
1955	31,649	43,601	75,250	57·9
1956	34,113	47,377	81,490	58·1
1957	35,098	48,611	83,709	58·1
1958	36,787	49,775	86,562	57·5
1959	38,792	50,871	89,663	56·7
1960	43,281	54,576	97,857	55·8
		Live births		
1961	48,490	59,115	107,605	54·9
1962	55,376	62,455	117,831	53·0
1963	59,104	64,427	123,531	52·2
1964	63,340	67,933	131,273	51·7
1965	66,249	70,457	136,706	51·5
1966	67,056	71,648	138,704	51·7
1967	69,928	73,667	143,595	51·3
1968	69,806	74,531	144,337	51·6
1969	67,041	72,595	139,636	52·0
1970	64,744	70,623	135,367	52·2
1971	65,678	67,294	132,972	50·6
Scotland				
		Live births†		
1955	3,991	5,756	9,747	59·1
1956	4,069	5,947	10,016	59·4
1957	4,017	5,851	9,868	59·3
1958	4,073	5,798	9,871	58·7
1959	4,134	5,939	10,073	59·0
1960	4,409	6,212	10,621	58·5
1961	4,648	6,152	10,800	57·0
1962	5,020	6,506	11,526	56·4
1963	5,340	6,441	11,781	54·7
1964	5,628	7,212	12,840	56·2
1965	5,883	7,184	13,067	55·0
1966	6,160	7,301	13,461	54·2
1967	6,663	7,747	14,410	53·8
1968	6,998	7,880	14,878	52·8
1969	6,727	8,101	14,828	54·6
1970	6,712	8,203	14,915	55·0
1971	7,028	7,998	15,026	53·2

* Legitimate live first births within 8 months of first marriage.
† In 1960 and earlier years the figures refer to first births in present marriage.

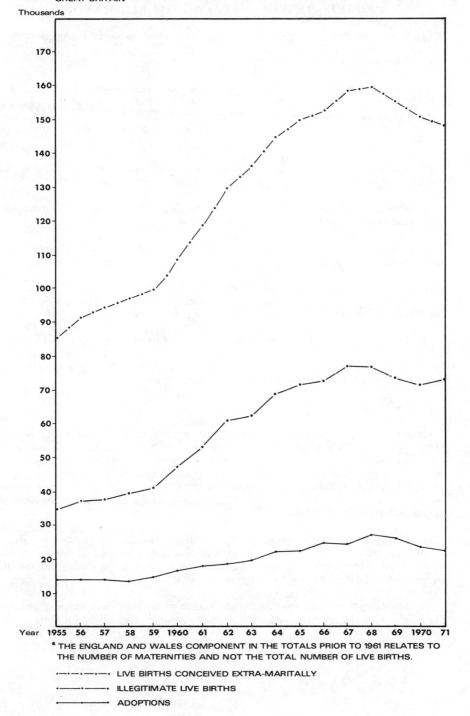

COMPARISON OF ADOPTIONS, ILLEGITIMATE LIVE BIRTHS*, AND LIVE BIRTHS
CONCEIVED EXTRA-MARITALLY*1955-1971
GREAT BRITAIN

Thousands

Year 1955 56 57 58 59 1960 61 62 63 64 65 66 67 68 69 1970 71

* THE ENGLAND AND WALES COMPONENT IN THE TOTALS PRIOR TO 1961 RELATES TO
THE NUMBER OF MATERNITIES AND NOT THE TOTAL NUMBER OF LIVE BIRTHS.

—·—·—·— LIVE BIRTHS CONCEIVED EXTRA-MARITALLY

·———·———· ILLEGITIMATE LIVE BIRTHS

———·——— ADOPTIONS

129

APPENDIX C

INFORMATION WHICH SHOULD BE REQUIRED OF VOLUNTARY ADOPTION SOCIETIES APPLYING FOR REGISTRATION

(a) *Address* of the society's administrative centre and addresses of any other offices.

(b) *Geographical* area to be covered.

(c) *Scope of activities and range of services proposed;* including the extent to which the society provides a general social work service for families (including unmarried parents), a general child care service, and casework with adoptive families; an indication of any special restrictive criteria in the acceptance of adopters, natural families or children.

(d) *Size of programme,* including actual numbers of placements in previous years and expected numbers in future.

(e) *Resources provided by the agency,* such as short-term accommodation for un-supported mothers, nursery and foster home facilities.

(f) *Resources available to the agency*—for example, by arrangement with other agencies: channels of communication with other relevant services e.g. housing, social security.

(g) *Financial resources,* sources of income, capital, fee-charging schemes; statement of accounts; whether the society applies the whole of its income in promoting the objects for which it exists; whether the society carries out any other activities.

(h) *Medical resources*—proposed arrangements for medical examination of child and adopters, and for medical assessment: names, qualifications, functions and availability of examiners and advisers; access to consultancy services including genetic, psychiatric and psychological services; co-ordination of medical aspects.

(i) *Legal resources*—arrangements for legal advice.

(j) *Agency staff*—details of the director and other workers, including clerical and supporting staff, with qualifications and experience of professional staff, and an indication of the proportion of their time spent on adoption work; adequacy of staffing for the work to be undertaken, including the additional responsibilities proposed for agencies in supervision of the child in the adoptive home and reporting to the court. Arrangements within the agency for staff consultation and supervision and the division of functions between professional workers and committee members.

(k) *Committee and case committee*—details of the constitution of the society; details of the members of the controlling committee, how the committee is appointed and exercises control; details of members of the case committee, with their qualifications and experience, and the activities of the committee.

(l) *Decision-making machinery* for the acceptance of adopters, acceptance of children for adoption, and placement; and the role of committee members and officers in this process.

APPENDIX D

SURVEYS OF CHILDREN RECLAIMED FROM CARE

Three separate surveys of children reclaimed or discharged from care were carried out by the Home Office for the Departmental Committee.

1. The first of the surveys, in which all local authorities in England and Wales took part, was carried out in 1968, before the Departmental Committee was set up. The purpose of the survey was to ascertain the number of children reclaimed by natural parents against the strong advice of the local authority during the year ending 31 March 1968, and to assess the effectiveness of section 2 of the Children Act 1948 for protecting children from removal from care when this seemed not to be in the child's best interest. (See paragraphs 3 to 5.)

2. The second was a survey of a random sample of local authorities and voluntary child care agencies to assess the number of children in care who had been in foster homes for a considerable period of time, and those who had been discharged from care after a considerable period in the same foster home. (See paragraphs 6 to 9.) The third was a follow-up of this second statistical survey, and consisted of a case analysis of three groups of children: those discharged from care after more than five years in the same foster home and those discharged after between two and five years, where the welfare of the child would, in the opinion of the agency, have been better served by his remaining in the foster home; and those children discharged after five years where, in the opinion of the agency, it was in the child's interests to go home. (See paragraphs 10 to 13.)

CHILDREN WITHDRAWN FROM CARE AGAINST LOCAL AUTHORITY ADVICE

3. In the year ending 31 March 1968, 455 children in the care of local authorities in England and Wales were reclaimed by their parents against the authority's strong advice. (The total number of children in the care of local authorities in England and Wales on 31 March 1968 was 69,358). These were children in care under section 1 of the Children Act 1948. Of the 455, only 66 had been continuously in care for two years or more (some 50 families). In the case of 18 of the 66 children, it was known that the foster parents wished to adopt the child, and in 17 of these 18 the local authority would have supported this. Of the 66 cases, the authority kept in touch with 53 children after their return home; in at least 16 cases, the child appeared to have settled satisfactorily. The survey did not identify the kind of care being provided for the children, and not all of the 66 were necessarily in foster homes.

4. The information given by the local authorities revealed some of the reasons why parents reclaimed their children, even after a considerable lapse of time. Sometimes a request to contribute financially to the child's maintenance may have precipitated the withdrawal. In a few cases, the child had reached working age. Sometimes an approach for consent to adoption seemed to precipitate the move. More often, however, the withdrawal of the child followed changes in circumstances in the natural family (often a solution of the original problem leading to the initial request for care), such as a marriage or remarriage, or rehousing. Some parents felt they could cope with their child once he was past babyhood. One authority commented that families with deep-seated problems often took five or six years to establish themselves; another, that some parents seemed to plan ahead consciously for the time when they would be in a position to have their child back.

5. Many authorities felt that the powers of section 2 of the Children Act 1948 were sufficient to protect children in care from being reclaimed against their interests. Others felt that the powers needed extending chiefly to protect children with inadequate and unstable parents and also where a parent suffered from intermittent mental illness, and where there were grounds for assuming parental rights against one parent but not against the other. In these kinds of cases, children tended to come in and out of care.

SURVEY OF CHILDREN IN FOSTER HOMES FOR A CONSIDERABLE PERIOD OF TIME

6. This was a survey, in a random sample of local authorities and in three voluntary child care agencies, of children in care on 31 December 1970 who had been in a foster home for a considerable period of time, and those discharged from care during the year ended 31 December 1970 after a considerable period in the same foster home. Its purpose was to obtain some indication of how many foster children might have been affected by propositions 16 and 21 in the Committee's working paper. 18 local authorities in England and Wales, 4 in Scotland, and 3 voluntary societies, were surveyed.

7. On 31 December, a total of 3,465 children in care of these 25 bodies had been boarded out in the same foster home for more than 5 years. A further 2,186 had been boarded out in the same foster home for more than 2 years and less than 5 years. 1,133 children had been in the same foster home for more than 1 year and less than 2 years.

8. During the year ended 31 December 1970, 38 children were discharged from care who had been in the same foster home for more than 5 years. 10 of these were under 1 year of age when boarded out. There was a wide scatter of age range among the children at discharge. In only 2 cases did the agency consider that it would have been in the interests of the child to remain in the foster home. One of these two children was aged 10 on discharge.

9. During the year, 74 children were discharged from care who had been in the same foster home for more than 2 years but less than 5. Of these, 14 children were under 1 year of age when boarded out. Of the 74 children, in only 14 cases did the agency consider that it would have been in the child's interests to remain in the foster home. It can be deduced from the returns that 6 of these 14 were not under 1 year of age when boarded out.

CASE ANALYSIS

10. Short case histories were submitted on 33 children (23 families) by agencies which participated in the statistical survey (paragraphs 6 to 9 above). These include 2 cases where children returned home after more than 5 years in a foster home where the agency considered that it might have been in the child's interest to stay in the foster home (first group); 5 cases (8 children) where the children were discharged after between 2 and 5 years in the same foster home, and where their interests might have been better served by remaining in the foster home (second group); and 15 cases (21 children) where the children returned home after more than 5 years in a foster home and where the agency felt that the return home was in the child's interests (third group). One case did not come within the time limits.

11. The case material revealed a number of children who returned home at adolescence, sometimes when nearing 18 years of age, mostly by their own decision. One younger adolescent acted impulsively by choosing to return home, and regretted it later. Section 2

132

rights to the agency could have protected this child against her own impulsive action. Other children returned home after quite a long period in the foster home where this had always been the plan, and contact with the natural family had been maintained. In many "typical" child care cases, a change in parental circumstances precipitated the withdrawal of the child—often a solution of the original problem leading to the need for care. In these cases, the parents took it for granted that the child would return home. In other cases, the fostering itself came to an end either because of changes in the foster home circumstances or with a breakdown in relationships between the child and the foster parents.

12. The case material revealed the very varied circumstances of these children. More-over, there was often no very clear-cut distinction between the first two groups and the third group of cases: in some cases in the first two groups the return home was inevitable and the less unsatisfactory of two solutions; in some cases in the third group, remaining in the foster home might well have been desirable. Difficult casework decisions sometimes had to be made, the child's long-term welfare often being far from easy to assess.

13. The material sent in by the agencies indicated considerable efforts made by social workers to work with natural families to retain contacts between children and families, and to plan ahead conscientiously for the children. Foster parents seem generally to have co-operated with the agency in plans for the child, even when this entailed parting with the child after a considerable period of time.

APPENDIX E

SUGGESTIONS FOR AN EXPLANATORY LEAFLET

We suggest in paragraph 183 that a leaflet explaining the two ways in which adoption arrangements can be made should be given to a mother wishing to have her child adopted. This leaflet will require careful preparation and in this Appendix we give only a suggested outline of it.

Explanatory leaflet

This leaflet explains the two ways in which arrangements may be made for your child to be adopted. It is for you to choose which you prefer.

A Relinquishing parental rights to an adoption agency

1. Under the first method the procedure is as follows. You and the agency jointly make a written application to the court to give up your rights and duties as a parent. These will be transferred to the adoption agency. The court will appoint a social worker to interview you and, if you confirm that you wish your child to be adopted, you will be able to sign a form, which the social worker will witness, agreeing to give up your rights and duties as a parent and to their transfer to the agency. (This form cannot be signed until the baby is at least six weeks old.) The social worker will tell you the place, date and time of the court hearing to consider your application. You need not go to the court and, if you do not, the court will be able to accept the written statement of your agreement to give up your rights as a parent. If you change your mind you may withdraw your application up to the time of the court hearing. But once the court has made the order transferring your rights and duties to the adoption agency this is final.

2. The adoption agency will place the child with prospective adopters who will, in due course, apply to a court for an adoption order. The adoption agency will be able to give consent to the adoption and you will not be involved.

3. Although it will be for the adoption agency to select the prospective adopters, they will keep in touch with you, if you wish, and will be able to tell you about the couple whom they have in mind as the new family for your child.

4. You may wonder what happens if the agency is unable to find adopters for your child. This is most unlikely, but if it should happen, the agency will retain responsibility for him and will arrange for his care in the best possible way. You would not be asked to have the child back yourself, but you may, if you wish, ask to be told what eventually happens so that you could have an opportunity of resuming care yourself if the child was not adopted.

B Consent to an adoption order by a particular couple

5. Under the second kind of procedure, the child is placed with prospective adopters, who tell the court that they intend to apply for an adoption order. The court appoints a social worker to interview you, as in the first procedure, and you are able to sign a written consent to adoption by that particular couple, which the social worker will witness. (You may not be told the names of the couple, if they prefer to remain anonymous.) When the prospective adopters apply to the court for an adoption order, they attach your written consent. Once this is done, you may not remove the child from their care without the permission of the court. An adoption order cannot be made unless the applicants have cared for the child for at least three months. In the meantime, you retain your rights and duties as a parent until the adoption order is made. When that is done, the adopters become, in law, the child's parents.

134

6. If, before the court hearing, you change your mind about adoption, you may withdraw your written consent by writing to say so or attending the court. But the court then has power, in certain circumstances, to dispense with your consent, and make an adoption order—for example, if it considers that you are withholding consent unreasonably. (In deciding whether you are withholding consent unreasonably a court is required by the law to have regard to all the circumstances, first consideration being given to the effect of your decision on the long-term welfare of the child.)

The choice of procedure is yours

7. The agency will explain to you the advantages and disadvantages of the two procedures, and suggest which is most appropriate in your case, but it is for you to choose.

Printed in England for Her Majesty's Stationery Office by McCorquodale Printers Ltd., London
HM 4829   Dd 141668   K 64   10/72